Playing for Celtic No 19

PLAYING FOR CELTIC NO19

Edited by Rodger Baillie

Stanley Paul

London Melbourne Auckland Johannesburg

Stanley Paul and Co. Ltd

An imprint of Century Hutchinson Ltd
Brookmount House, 62–65 Chandos Place
Covent Garden, London WC2N 4NW

Century Hutchinson Australia (Pty) Ltd
PO Box 496, 16–22 Church Street, Hawthorn, Melbourne, Victoria 3122

Century Hutchinson New Zealand Limited
191 Archers Road, PO Box 40–086, Glenfield, Auckland 10

Century Hutchinson South Africa (Pty) Ltd
PO Box 337, Bergvlei 2012, South Africa

First published 1987
Copyright © Stanley Paul and Co. Ltd 1987

Set in Baskerville by Deltatype Ltd, Ellesmere Port, South Wirral

Printed and bound by Anchor Brendon Ltd, Tiptree, Essex

British Cataloguing in Publication Data

Playing for Celtic. — No. 19
  1.   Glasgow Celtic Football Club — Periodicals
  796.334'63'0941443   GV943.6.G/

ISBN 0 09 171301 3

Black and white photographs by Sportapics, Syndication International and *Celtic View*
Colour photographs by Colorsport, Sportapics and Syndication International

Frontispiece: Stretch! Celtic keeper Pat Bonner tips
over a Rangers effort in an Old Firm match

CONTENTS

RETURN OF THE PRODIGAL

Scottish football has never known a season like it! The headlines on and off the field forced soccer frequently away from the back page on to the front page. The pace was set by Rangers, who were to end as the new Premier League champions, before the season started with their big-money buys of English internationals Terry Butcher and Chris Woods. But if Rangers took the giant share of the headlines – critics sometimes complained too big a share – every other major side was also involved.

Celtic were hit by the death of veteran director Tom Devlin, shortly after he had presided at the unfurling of the Premier League championship flag, and he was replaced by Jack McGinn in the key role of chairman.

There was the controversy about whether Celtic should travel to Kiev to fulfil their European Cup tie, because the city was so close to the site of the nuclear power station disaster at Chernobyl. There was the stormy Skol Cup Final between Celtic and Rangers; a battle between the Old Firm as they fought for league supremacy, with the Ibrox side chipping away an apparently impregnable Parkhead lead. And, as far as Celtic were concerned, for much of the season two off-the-field situations seemed to dominate – the failure to sign new players went hand-in-hand with an apparently endless saga of whether or not first Mo Johnston and then Brian McClair would re-sign. In the event Celtic lost their strike force with Johnston announcing he would sign for French club, Nantes, days after McClair had indicated he was joining Manchester United. Alan McInally decided that he, too, would leave Parkhead.

Murdo MacLeod was another to quit, joining West German team, Borussia Dortmund, although Celtic made it clear that while, especially in Johnston's case, they were unhappy with the role of players' agents, the long-serving mid-field man had kept Celtic informed fully of his plans.

The new manager of Celtic . . . Billy McNeill

Dundee United, who had earlier lost assistant manager Walter Smith and striker Davie Dodds, were forced to transfer key defender Richard Gough to Spurs. They recovered so well they earned the praise of the whole nation as they won their way to the final of the UEFA Cup Final, only to lose to Swedish side Gothenburg on aggregate – five days after they had been defeated by St Mirren in the Scottish Cup Final.

Aberdeen lost their sheet anchor when manager Alex Ferguson moved to Manchester United taking assistant Archie Knox with him, and the Pittodrie club had difficulty in finding a successor until they appointed Ian Porterfield. Hearts had moved quickly to block a possible Aberdeen move for assistant manager Sandy Jardine, by moving him up to co-manager with Alex MacDonald.

City rivals Hibs sacked manager John Blackley, and replaced him with St Mirren's Alex Miller – but not before there had been suggestions the man they really wanted was Celtic's Davie Hay. And at Paisley when Alex Smith took over from Miller he and his assistant Jimmy Bone guided St Mirren to their first Scottish Cup victory for twenty-eight years.

Dundee United's neighbours, Dundee, had been so long in the shadow of their once unfashionable neighbours. The frustration of influential fans was felt when there were two unsuccessful take-over bids.

And at international level new team boss Andy Roxburgh discovered that managing Scotland was a far more difficult task than his previous role of only coaching. A miserable statistical record of only one victory in seven matches – with the other six split between three defeats and three draws – and just four goals scored marked one of Scotland's unhappiest international seasons. It was a disappointing season both for Roxburgh and Celtic skipper Roy Aitken, picked as the skipper of the international side right through the series of games.

The curtain rang down on a season which also had the longest programme of domestic matches – with the Premier League reshaped to stretch to forty-four fixtures – when Scotland were beaten 2–0 by a young and promising Brazil side at Hampden.

And the sensational news announced in the early evening of Thursday, 28 May, was that Celtic had sacked their manager, David Hay, and replaced him with Billy McNeill, the man who had himself left the club controversially in 1983. It was only twenty days previously that McNeill had himself faced the sack, as manager of relegated Aston Villa who went down to the English Second Division along with Manchester City, the club Billy had moved to when he left Parkhead and whom he had left to switch to Birmingham only in the previous September.

Scotland's star Player of the Year, Brian McClair, celebrates one of his many individual awards in champagne style – the *Daily Record*'s prize for the first player in Scotland last season to hit 30 domestic goals

As Celtic chairman Jack McGinn said: 'We are glad to welcome back the prodigal son.' The pieces of the jigsaw of the amazing change were then pieced together. The Parkhead club had been negotiating on a close-season tour of Australia, finally declared off on that fateful Thursday morning. When Hay was called back to the ground early in the afternoon to meet the chairman he apparently thought it was because yet again there had been a change of plan for the tour. Instead it was to be told he was to go, and Jack McGinn said later: 'I feel sorry for Davie because he is a nice guy. It was the worst thing I've ever had to do, to tell him what the board had decided.

'Davie took the news as I had expected, with obvious disappointment but with dignity. I am saddened by what has happened, and I honestly hope I never have to do it again.'

From Ibrox there came a statement by Rangers boss Graeme Souness who said: 'My thoughts go out to Davie Hay at this moment. I regarded him as a personal friend and I hope I never have to suffer what he must be going through at the moment.' And Billy McNeill, who only those few short weeks before had been in the same position as Hay, said: 'I feel sorry for Davie Hay. I know what it is like to lose a job; my memory of this is very fresh.'

For McNeill it was an incredible turn-around to return to the club he had left so controversially when he fell out with the late chairman, Desmond White. Yet just as some in football are always associated with one club – Bill Shankly with Liverpool, Bill Nicholson with Spurs, Willie Waddell with Rangers – so surely is Billy McNeill linked with Celtic.

His association with Parkhead had begun in 1957, when he was signed for the massive sum of £250, and he had gone on to win every domestic honour, topped by the marvellous time when he skippered Celtic to the European Cup Final victory in Lisbon against Inter Milan in 1967.

McNeill's love of Celtic shone through at an impromptu speech I heard him make at a private lunch to celebrate that Lisbon victory. The listening Celtic directors could hardly have failed to be impressed. The deal to bring him back was settled in a car park at Clydebank and Billy returned to tell a press conference: 'When I was asked to take the job it took me all of two seconds to make up my mind. Celtic have been my life. I joined them as a boy, and now I'm back as manager for the second time. Any acrimony is in the past. I want to look to the future. There has never been any other club for me, despite my move to England.

'I even think being sacked by Villa will do me good. It is part of my education and I hope the end product will be good for Celtic.'

And he made it clear Celtic would aim to topple Rangers from their position as the new kings of Scottish football. 'I'll be challenging Graeme Souness in the next year, and I think Celtic can finish on top. Rangers have set a standard and it is up to us to better this. I admire what he has done since he went to Ibrox, although I'll try to do things in a different way. But I want the balance of power to return to Parkhead.'

A sorry sight for Celtic fans, as Mo Johnston, right foot in plaster, hobbles into Glasgow Airport after cutting short a pre-season tour of Ireland and is met by reporter Rodger Baillie

King of Parkhead . . . Brian McClair, the scoring hero of the season

Billy praised Hay's signing of Republic of Ireland defender Mick McCarthy from Manchester City, the same player McNeill himself had bought from Barnsley for the Maine Road club. He talked about his own sacking from Aston Villa and said: 'I was in despair. I had no idea Celtic would want me back. I was never very far away from them in exile. I looked at their result first every week and, of course, my pals in Glasgow kept me in touch.'

So the changeover was completed. It was only just over two weeks since the last league game of the season, a 1–0 defeat by Hearts at Tynecastle. Then thousands of loyal Celtic fans had waited on the terraces cheering for their heroes, but it was twenty

The power of Alan McInally, as he scores in the 6–0 victory against Clydebank at Parkhead

minutes before they appeared. The players were kept behind in the dressing-room getting an after-match rollicking from Hay. I never saw a more grim-faced bunch of players when they finally appeared to wave to their supporters. And in the last interview I had with him as Celtic manager Hay told me: 'Perhaps I should have done it more often.' I recalled that the boss of the double-glazing firm C.R. Smith, when announcing the terms of a new sponsorship contract, had said: 'Perhaps it puts more pressure on Mr Hay.' More in earnest than as a joke the Celtic manager had replied: 'That's nothing new.'

The demands for success are now so intense that we will never see again the long reigns of such men as Willie Maley at Celtic or Bill Struth with Rangers, the founding fathers of the managerial dynasties at both clubs. Even the comparatively recent stints of Jock Stein, 13 years at Parkhead, or Scot Symon, one year longer at Ibrox, will not be repeated.

Hay's sacking, just as the year before when Jock Wallace left Rangers, showed that neither half of the Old Firm can afford not to be successful. The test for the manager of each club is how many trophies his side can win to preserve his job.

So Celtic, founded in 1888, are still going strong despite all the ups and downs of football as they approach their centenary year. Yet there are drumbeats of doubt in the background, as their nearest rivals, Rangers, have revolutionized Scotland's soccer scene in the last season.

For better or worse things will never be the same again. I cannot agree with those who claim it is the greatest test the rest of football has ever faced. That is the same over-emphasized claim made by politicians that every General Election is the most vital the country has ever faced. Nevertheless the challenge from Ibrox, so obviously designed to put a stranglehold on trophy winning, does present a demanding situation.

Some supporters have claimed Celtic should become a public limited company, to attempt to match Rangers at financial level. In this book chairman Jack McGinn states his opposition to such a scheme. Time will tell if his thinking, and that of the present board of directors is correct.

The end of the season also closed the curtain on one of the great careers of Scottish football, the twenty-year stint of long service defender Danny McGrain had given Celtic. Captain of Celtic, captain of Scotland. A battler off the field as well as on it who had recovered from a fractured skull and illness caused by diabetes Danny admitted: 'I suppose I'm as rare as the dinosaur, for full-back is a disappearing position in modern football.' He is also rare in the loyalty he gave one club, a disappearing commodity in a soccer world increasingly dominated by agents trying to manipulate the best contract packages for their playing clients.

McGrain was given a free transfer, but the manner of his departure even though at the age of thirty-seven it could hardly have been delayed much longer, showed an insensitivity from a club who have long proclaimed their promotion of a family atmosphere inside the team.

So season 1986–87 was one of disappointment. There was a chink of light for the future in the winning of the BP Youth Cup, with victory against Motherwell in the final.

But Celtic's top team had a melancholy catalogue. Second in

14

The perfect tackle from a perfect defender – Danny McGrain, in his last season for Celtic, takes the ball away from Aberdeen teenage striker Paul Wright

the Premier League, defeated Skol Cup finalists, defeated Glasgow Cup finalists, out of the Scottish Cup and the European Champions Cup, although in mitigation they earned praise for their performance in Russia in the last-named trophy from SFA secretary Ernie Walker in his annual report.

However, a study of Celtic's proud hundred-year history shows that such set-backs in the past have served as a major spur to glory again. No one should doubt the powerful resolve of the new Celtic manager to add another glittering chapter to that history in the club's centenary season!

THE LONELIEST JOB
by Davie Hay

The season had ended. But for Davie Hay the term 'close-season' simply did not exist. It was a time of wheeling and dealing in the transfer market, attempting to repair the gaps that had shone so despairingly at times during the season.

As we talked, with interruptions from ringing phones and personal callers, he leaned back in his chair and admitted:

'This is the loneliest job in the world. I remember when I was a player at Chelsea being on a close-season tour and Eddie McCreadie who was then the manager at Stamford Bridge saying that. I really didn't know what he meant by it . . . but I do now.

'Maybe you have to experience all we've gone through this season to make you a harder person. All I know is that it will make me a better manager.'

Unfortunately for Davie Hay the verdict on that would not be given at Parkhead. The following week the Celtic board sacked him, and he was replaced by Billy McNeill.

It had been a punishing, demanding season, made even harder by Celtic's failure to win any of the top four trophies for which they competed.

Hay looked back over the four competitions and gave his end-of-term verdicts.

SKOL CUP: We started with wins against Airdrie and Dumbarton, and then we met Aberdeen at Pittodrie.

We always knew away from home it would be tight, but as we progressed there were more incidents and controversy.

The fact the Aberdeen match went to penalties summed up the type of game it was. However getting through at such a hard place as Pittodrie made us hope we had a chance of winning the trophy.

We didn't play well against Motherwell in the semi-final, we even conceded a two-goal lead. It took another penalty decider to win us the place in the final, where we met Rangers.

Happier times for Davie Hay as he returns from a Celtic trip, as a player, with team-mates Jim Brogan (*left*) and Danny McGrain

What happened during that game has been well catalogued, and as I don't want to appear before the SFA again I'd better not repeat some of my earlier remarks.

It was a tight, tense match and although Rangers went in front I thought we had a chance through that great goal of Brian McClair's. However the penalty award swung it Rangers' way, and the events after that have been well discussed.

But looking back now it had a bearing on how the rest of the campaign went. Although we were ahead in the league at that time it gave Rangers an edge because they felt they had the beating of us, at least in the games between our two teams.

I feel if we had beaten Rangers that day we would have gained in strength and, at a time when they were trailing us, they might have suffered a blow that would have taken them time to recover from.

THE EUROPEAN CUP: We played Shamrock Rovers in the first round, and although the score on aggregate over the two games was not large it was still a comfortable 3–0 victory.

The next side we drew was Dynamo Kiev, surely one of the hardest club sides in the entire range of European tournaments. It was a mystery they did not end the season as winners of the European Cup.

Again a slack goal cost us dearly and we suffered the loss of Tommy Burns in that game at Parkhead, one of the major body blows of the entire season. However we equalized, and in fact in the second game in Kiev it looked as if we were going to win at one stage, because we had the upper hand in the second half.

It was not to be, but I felt the display, especially by some of our youngsters, gave us a bit of hope for the future.

SCOTTISH CUP: We played four matches in the tourney, but only got through one round. That was because we had one match, and then two replays, against Aberdeen.

We produced three first-class performances in the games. Ironically one of the best displays of the entire second half of the season was in the second replay against the Dons at Dens Park, where we had our worst league game.

I don't know if these games took a toll on the players, but I'm not offering that as any excuse. They should have got a lift from the result.

The next round was no easier, a formidable tie against Hearts at Tynecastle. It looked as if it would go to a replay when John Robertson scored for them in the last period of the game and we were out of the Cup.

Happier times for Davie Hay as he and Jock Wallace, then manager of Rangers, enjoy a cuppa before catching European flights

PREMIER LEAGUE: This was our biggest disappointment, and one game for me highlighted all our season's problems. That was the match against Dundee at Dens Park, when we led 1–0 at the interval and at the same time Rangers were trailing to Hibs at Ibrox. Yet we ended up on the wrong end of a 4–1 score-line. It epitomized the rights and wrongs of the season . . . and that day it was the wrongs that took centre-stage.

The New Year's Day game when Rangers beat us 2–0 at Ibrox was another disaster. It gave them a marvellous lift, but we fell away after that.

David Hay was characteristically blunt about the problems.

'We ended the season as top scorers, but basically it was the number of goals we conceded which caused all the trouble.

'Celtic have an attacking style, which to a degree you can't change and, anyway, that has been the trademark of the club for so long it would be wrong to alter it. But that shouldn't account for the amount or the manner in which we lost goals, and which cost us the League.'

He touched on the failure to bring new players to Parkhead during the season and said: 'The best time would have been the close-season, but for whatever reasons, we didn't do it. We made a greater push at the turn of the year, and in fact before it, but the availability was just not there and caused us extra worries.'

There were problems on the field as well for Hay admitted: 'We can reach peaks higher than anyone but then we go down a bit lower than we should with the standard of players we've got. And because we lose goals too easily an edge creeps into our play and filters through the whole team.'

He warned: 'Unless we eradicate this problem the same thing will occur again.

'Yet at the start of the season we thought we had sorted it out, with only six goals lost in the first ten games. But that can't hide the fact that overall it was the goals conceded which cost us our chance of winning a trophy.'

There were other disappointments as well: 'Some of the younger players didn't make the breakthrough for which we had hoped. But having said that one or two of the experienced players didn't show the consistency expected of them.

'We are a young side and to keep asking them to produce top-class displays every week is maybe too much.'

Hay also expressed the same criticism so many managers feel about the length of the programme.

'Admittedly it's the same for all the teams at the top, the sides who hope to do well in Europe and in the two Cups, Scottish and Skol.

'But add international commitments to that and the simple fact is there are too many games.

'Look at the Scottish Cup Final, and the effect it had on Dundee United who have been trying to battle on three fronts, Europe, Premier League and the Scottish Cup. They looked a jaded side, simply because of the number of games involved.

Happier times for Davie Hay as he lines up with his squad for the team picture before the start of season 1986–87

'It affects the players physically, and it gets to the stage that you wonder if it's too much for the pockets of the fans as well. Certainly it's an awful lot of games.'

The Hay end-of-season report on Celtic was one echoed by so many of the team's fans. . . 'We could have done better,' he said.

However Davie Hay is not someone to be taken on lightly!

He showed considerable courage during the season in one controversial area on which it would have been easy for him as manager to take a less than public stance. That was the storm which arose over Celtic players blessing themselves in public on the pitch during a game. The manager was incensed when sections of the crowd started chanting for players to perform an act which he saw as sacred, and not a response to idiotic terracing chants.

He spoke out publicly, and in my view correctly, about the practice and took the flak which came his way, although it was far outweighed by the approval he was given, not least by the Catholic Church itself.

Hay also showed courage at the loutish behaviour of some fans who chucked supporters' scarves at him at moments of defeat. I remember particularly the long walk at Dens Park from the dug-out to the dressing-room ramp on that awful day when Celtic

Davie Hay joins forces with Rangers star Davie Cooper (*second left, front row*) to meet some of the Ex-Servicemen at the Erskine Home

were thumped by Dundee. But the defeat did not justify the behaviour of those scarf-throwing fans. Davie Hay was just as annoyed as them about the team's display. Yet he confined himself to a brief comment about 'Un-Celtic behaviour' at the after-match press conference.

Naturally in a season which he described as 'a big disappointment' it is easy to concentrate on the days, or nights, when the results went against Celtic. But there were other moments to remember, such as the Cup wins against Aberdeen and the Parkhead victory against Rangers.

But there were not enough of them to save the Celtic managerial career of the quiet man who paid the penalty for those trophy failures last season.

MY PLAN FOR KEEPERS
by Pat Bonner

Football as a spectator sport has been around long enough to be encrusted with myths, the sort of statements made with such sweeping certainty for so long no one ever bothers to question them. One of them surrounds the men who occupy the Number One jersey in any team, and has been handed down from generation to generation accompanied by much nodding of the collective heads.

It goes along the lines that all good goalkeepers have to be 'daft'. Perhaps it sprang from the fact that traditionally there has been a touch of showmanship about keepers, perhaps it arose because there is a masochistic streak in those who happily hurl themselves into the churned-up stretches of mud that pass for goalmouths during much of the winter.

Whatever the reasons, I have always felt it a cruel slur on keepers for, personally speaking after nearly thirty years as a football reporter, I have never found them as a body to contain in their number any more of those who could be tagged as eccentric, than for example, wingers.

Certainly anyone who has ever spent a few minutes in the company of Celtic's current Number One choice, Pat Bonner, would immediately realize he is someone with firm, positive views on a wide range of soccer subjects.

He talks with considerable expertise, for instance, on the way goalkeepers are groomed. Pat finds the present system wanting, and is not afraid to speak out about it: 'Young goalkeepers are not taught the right things; maybe if they had good tutors it would be easier for them. They might get coaching when they are twenty or twenty-one, and by then it's so much harder to iron out the mistakes in their style of play.

'I don't believe for a minute all the criticism that is made on TV about Scottish keepers. But there's no doubt that with proper coaching they could be made better. As it is, far too many goalkeepers are simply asked to do the same sort of training as outfield players, with no real provision for their special needs.'

Scotland manager Andy Roxburgh has made a start with

special coaching for the country's top keepers by Englishman Alan Hodgkinson. But Bonner has a sensible and wide-ranging scheme which he claims would raise standards.

'The keepers at part-time clubs in the League should be coached on a regular basis by the top keepers in the country.

'Just think of it, Jim Leighton of Aberdeen, Dundee United's Billy Thomson and Bobby Geddes of Dundee looking after the north, Henry Smith of Hearts and Alan Rough of Hibs in the east, Chris Woods of Rangers and myself and some others in the west.

'That's the way it should be started, with the ones at the top branching out and everybody getting some tuition.'

Pat admits: 'I never really had any coaching. I picked up the odd hint when the Irish team were training. But no one was ever around to tell me the way it was done at the top level.

'I'm sure Chris Woods benefited from the help Peter Shilton must have given him. He was taught properly when he was young, and it stayed that way. But most of us had to learn the hard way, simply by our own mistakes.

'Really I feel if the youngsters of fifteen to seventeen get good

Ouch! Pat Bonner goes through the pain barrier as, assisted by Paul McGugan, he tries to stop Rangers skipper Terry Butcher

Dive! Celtic skipper Roy Aitken guards Pat Bonner as Rangers striker Ally McCoist races in

habits the standard of goalkeeping will improve. It's a shame so many kids simply don't get the chance to do better.'

Pat Bonner has put his ideas into practice for the past two years over in his native County Donegal, with a scheme involving sixteen high schools in the area with one budding keeper selected from each school for special coaching.

'It's something I never had when I was young, and hopefully I'm putting something into the place where I was brought up. But I really do think it should be set up on a much bigger scale. I feel sorry for kids who struggle as a keeper because they never have had the right coaching.

'And in Glasgow, especially, having to play on ash parks is no joke, landing on such a rock-hard surface. You can still be picking the red blaize bits out from your legs and arms a week later, and I'm sure kids get fed up.'

The Celtic keeper believes that the last line in the team has become a more glamorous position for youngsters than they once regarded it.

'We're not exactly at the stage of resembling American footballers, but I think one of the major differences in the ten years

25

I've been a senior keeper is the vast improvement in the equipment I wear.'

Pat recalls ruefully: 'When I came to Celtic at first I remember going to train at Coltness Juniors ground, with the other two keepers on the staff, Peter Latchford and Roy Baines. It was the first time I had ever to save shots from professional players, and although I had on the gloves I normally wore I still had lumps taken out of my hands for they just weren't good enough for the job.'

He looks back on the improvements that have been made and remembers: 'Peter Latchford started to wear cricket gloves, and then Peter McCloy sponge rubber gloves.

'Now the sports manufacturers are happy to let a keeper design his own individual kit, even to the style of the jersey and the type of gloves he wants.

'Once you've started wearing gloves you wouldn't be without them. You just don't feel right unless you have got them for every game. They really do improve tremendously the grip on the ball.'

But Pat also disclosed that on very hard grounds he wears extra protection for his elbows, with a padding similar to that used by the contestants in kick boxing.

'Knocks on the elbow are the worst thing in the world. If it happens repeatedly it causes a condition we call jelly elbow, which results in painful swelling.'

Goalkeepers' shorts now are padded to ease the pain of landing on hard surfaces, and Pat predicts: 'The first thigh pads have been designed with shock-absorbent foam so maybe they will become a big seller eventually.'

He stresses: 'The more protection a keeper has the more confident he will be during a game. Take Dundee United's Billy Thomson who always wears tracksuit bottoms because he feels they give him extra protection and he's more comfortable in them.

'At the end of the day as long as he keeps goal well, who cares what he wears?'

Goalkeepers as a breed tend to be more clannish. The keeper's mafia I do believe exists, and they welcome their rivals into it.

Rangers' Chris Woods, an English international, is accepted by the other keepers in Scotland for as Pat says: 'I'm sure his arrival gave us all a lift, for I know I looked on Chris coming to Scotland as a spur to myself and I wasn't the only one who regarded it in that light.

'I reckon the likes of Jim Leighton, Billy Thomson, Henry Smith and Bobby Geddes all had better seasons because Rangers signed Chris Woods.

'Rangers paid a fortune for him, so Chris knew he had to do

Reach! Pat Bonner makes a valiant attempt to clear the ball from the Celtic danger zone as Ibrox stars Ally McCoist and Terry Butcher challenge

well, and it was an incentive to the rest of us with a challenge we all took up.'

Like Woods with England the Celtic keeper is now a regular for his country, the Republic of Ireland. Yet it is a role Pat has not won without a long struggle.

As he explained: 'The previous international manager of Ireland Eion Hand never came over to watch games in Scotland when I was playing with Celtic.

'I believe I was always judged in the past in Ireland on matches on TV, and most of them were the clips shown on the lunch-time programmes on a Saturday.

'But because these inevitably show goals scored then it's the poor old keeper who is picking the ball out of the back of the net.

Hold it! Celtic's Pat Bonner outjumps friend and foe, the Celtic defence and Dundee United's attackers, as he moves to catch the ball

They very rarely show the saves a keeper makes, only when he loses a goal.

'And it's even harder for the keepers of Celtic or Rangers. If either of us make mistakes they are magnified simply because we are on TV nearly every week, certainly three times out of the four Saturdays in a month.

'Top keepers in England simply don't have that sort of spotlight on them, and I think it creates a false impression.'

Despite the TV concentration on the Old Firm Bonner is now firmly established as Ireland's first choice. He says: 'I had a few games before Jack Charlton, but until then I always felt it difficult to make the right impression.

'He's a very good manager who knows what he wants, and that was shown when we beat Scotland at Hampden. His pre-match reading of what would happen was simply superb.

'He told us how the Scots would play, and how we were to go out to overcome them. And it worked out the way he said it would.

The keeper who is as pleased as the fans, Celtic's Pat Bonner shows his jubilation at a Mo Johnston goal at the other end of the park

That sort of situation makes a team really confident about their manager.'

There is one other extra bonus when international dates come round now, for Pat is no longer on the sidelines. As he says: 'I had travelled so often just to be a reserve it became a standing joke with the other lads at Celtic Park.

'I felt I should have played, and I desperately wanted to get on and show the folks back home I was good enough for the international team.

'Now it's nice to be really involved and come back and talk to my Celtic team-mates about international games.'

But, of course, that was not the main topic among the Celtic players last season, it was the race for the League championship which they eventually lost to Rangers. Says Pat: 'We had a fantastic start with everything going great, but I felt we were always under pressure, from the fans and especially from the press for not signing players.

'No one really said we had done well to stay where we were, there always seemed to be controversy that the team wasn't good enough.

'Eventually we did drop points, and there were injury worries. Tommy Burns was out for a very long time, Murdo MacLeod had a spell on the sidelines and Roy Aitken was moved into midfield.

'We had some very young lads in the defence. I'm sure they will all benefit from the experience of last season.'

The Mo Johnston re-signing saga became as regular an event as the twice-weekly screening of 'Eastenders' and Bonner said: 'It definitely did affect us. Some of us also had contracts to discuss and when the club put a brake on any negotiations until the end of the season after Mo's business had dragged on and on it was unsettling.

'Yet at the end of it all we gave Rangers a run for their money. I still think we were desperately unlucky in the Skol Cup Final where we were the better team on the day. And we were doubly unfortunate because at that time we went out of the European Cup in Kiev, again by a narrow margin.

'Looking back over the season we did better than Dundee United or Aberdeen, but we know it's no use for Celtic to be second best.'

Pat's decision to re-sign for the club was a bright flame of good news amidst the end of season gloom about players planning to leave. He says: 'I believe Celtic fans are more loyal than anywhere else. We must have a bit of pride in the club, for we know we should be up there at the very top.'

Certainly as the club had no other recognized first-team keeper

Big night out, as Celtic's mascot marches out for the Roy Aitken
testimonial match, accompanied by Manchester United skipper Bryan
Robson and Pat Bonner

on their books after Peter Latchford's release it would have been a
devastating blow if Bonner had not re-signed.

He can look back on nearly ten years at Parkhead, and the
changes – not just in their mode of dress – which have affected
goalkeepers. He tells me: 'When I look at clips of old games it
always amazes me to see the keeper kicking out, with the defenders
standing behind him. That changed, especially with full-backs
sometimes being almost the same as wingers. Then came the
four-step rule; indeed at one stage there seemed to be change in the
laws of the game regarding keepers almost every year.

'Personally I feel sure the next major step will be a four-second
rule to make sure keepers do not hold the ball longer than that
before they release it.

'It's designed to speed up the game and I once played under a
referee who apparently on his own initiative, applied the rule in a
pre-season match in West Germany.'

However, no matter what rule changes are made, it's certain
that the big Irishman from Donegal will be able to cope as he
keeps goal for Celtic. Pat and team-mate Pierce O'Leary have
formed a cleaning company in Glasgow which they call 'Safe
Hands' – and there couldn't be a better title!

MAN AT THE TOP

No chairman of a major football club can expect a life of relaxation in the competitive soccer atmosphere of the eighties. The list of problems which can spring up for the leader of a top club seems to cover more areas of responsibility than even the Secretary of State for Scotland has to worry about.

The modern-day chairman is expected to be an expert on everything from crowd safety to the quality of food served in the club executive restaurant. But surely few chief executives have had a more daunting baptism than Celtic's new chairman, Jack McGinn.

He was made vice-chairman in the summer of 1986, and only a few months later was appointed chairman after the untimely death of Tom Devlin, who had been in the post for just over a year. He was soon plunged into a series of dramatic controversies that would have tested the nerve of the most experienced chairman.

Celtic were drawn against the Russian side Dynamo Kiev, with their base so close to the scene of the nuclear power-station disaster at Chernobyl. Then came the controversial Skol Cup final and the long-drawn-out re-signing drama of Mo Johnston coupled with the club's attempts and failures to sign new players.

No wonder, as we sat last spring and looked back on his opening spell in office, the new chairman said: 'One thing happened after another. I genuinely believe we could not get a six-month spell like it again. I don't doubt there will be difficult times, and there will be plenty of problems along the way. But I'm certain they will never be backed up, one against the other, in such a fashion again.

'It seemed we hardly got rid of one problem before another one arrived to take its place.'

One of the most awkward to deal with was the European Cup pairing with the Russians, for the threat of a health risk to the travelling party was not to be lightly discounted.

Admitted Jack McGinn: 'You would ask six different experts if it was safe to go there, and they would all come up with slightly different answers.

'Eventually the consensus was in favour of us going and I had to convince the players there was no danger.

The new men at the top . . . manager Billy McNeill and chairman Jack McGinn

'I had meetings with them in dressing-rooms and I told them if there was the slightest element of risk I wasn't going, and I wasn't asking anyone else to go either.'

But the genuine fears persisted among the players and the chairman revealed: 'One or two almost didn't go.'

He went on: 'The worst part for me was when the food we had promised the players we would take with us disappeared on arrival at Kiev Airport. I genuinely thought then that some of the team would demand to get right back on the plane and fly back to Glasgow.

'The Russians assured us if we went on to the hotel the food would follow. Maybe I've been conditioned by too many spy novels, but I didn't completely believe them.

'Eventually they agreed to let us put it onto wagons which would go with the team bus, and I even helped to load it up to make sure we had no hitches.'

That episode, and many of the other headaches, must have seemed a very long way from his childhood for the man, who like thousands of children in the past hundred years, had been reared in a Celtic environment.

Joked Jack McGinn: 'I suppose I was a Celtic supporter more or less at birth. Certainly my father and brothers were keen on

Celtic. In fact it was probably the main topic of conversation in the house.

'My father was a quite exceptional billiards player, although I never saw him in his prime. The manager of Celtic at the time, Willie Maley, knew him and asked him to interest his sons in the sport. As a result he was fairly friendly with Willie Maley whom I met once or twice although I couldn't really claim to know him because he was a pretty old man by then.'

Jack McGinn states with conviction: 'I was interested in Celtic from the time I knew anything about football,' and he certainly didn't hesitate when I asked him who was his boyhood idol in the team.

'My outstanding favourite was Malcolm McDonald and he possibly still is to this day. Perhaps it was a question of seeing him through a youngster's eyes but to me he seemed the most complete footballer I had ever seen.

'Yet I never saw him in his prime, only at the end of the war years not long before he left Celtic Park. Of course he played in every position, but most of the time I saw him he was in the old right-half position. He had been signed, I believe, as a centre-half and although he was only 5ft 8in tall he was immense in the air.

'My abiding memory is of his complete ability. He had two great feet, terrific balance and I can recall clearly seeing him often bring a ball down on the edge of the six-yards line, swerve past a couple of players from the opposition and deliver a great pass to a team-mate, and all the time he was in total control.

'For any youngster interested in the game Malcolm McDonald bordered on perfection.'

Another famous Celt of the time, winger Jimmy Delaney, was a hero of the schoolboy Jack McGinn.

The young man came through the traditional assembly line of schools football and Boys' Guild football, and had a spell at Leeds United, then in the English Second Division. They had already made one signing, the man who was to become their most famous player of that period, just as the fifties started – John Charles. The manager, Major Frank Buckley, had made his name pre-war with Wolverhampton Wanderers and, as a forerunner of the more famous 'Busby Babes' at Manchester United, the young players he was signing at Elland Road were known as the 'Buckley Babes'.

Recalls Jack McGinn: 'He was a forbidding, austere person, who was so remote you only saw him if he wanted to see you. He bore no resemblance to any football manager nowadays.

'Occasionally at practice games he had this weird habit of sitting in the stand with a microphone attached to the loudspeaker system, and believe me, he could give players pelters. If you got a

Jack McGinn, the man who took over as Celtic chairman during season 1986–87

ball, went past a defender and then knocked it over the bar instead of across the goal he would blast out his annoyance over the tannoy.

'I was probably a bit of a tanner ba' player and this did not go down well. Behind Elland Road's main stand there was a great big area of black ash we used as a training pitch; as I remember there weren't even any goal-posts up.

'I used to like to get the ball and nick in and about people, although I was constantly told that wasn't what was expected of me. I was supposed to make a pass as soon as I got the ball.

'One of the coaches was Frank Taylor, a former Wolves player, and he used to tell me on the quiet to get on and play the way I wanted.

'However I wasn't really very happy, and after spells at home then back at Leeds I finally called it a day.'

But Jack vividly remembers the impact the giant John Charles made at the start of a career that was to make his such a famous name. Later he became one of the first of the big-name exports to the Continent when he joined Italian side, Juventus.

'John had just turned 18 and went off to do his National Service, and win his first Welsh cap. His brother Mel was also on Leeds' books, and the general opinion at the time was that he was only there because of John.

'That shows how wrong people can be about players. Mel eventually became a top-line star through his own ability and not his brother's reflected glory.'

The Celtic chairman looks back on that period and says: 'I suppose it was the start of the change from ten outfield players just running about. A bit more thought went into tactics, but it took a lot longer in Scotland.

'Traditionally until then the best players were the wing-halves or inside-forwards so they were always picked to play there. You looked for pace from wingers, a bit of bravery to put the ball in the back of the net from the centre-forward, a big guy at centre-half and the fellows who weren't quite good enough for anything else were the two full-backs. If the goalkeeper looked as if he might be able to stop the ball at all then he was in.

'And it was a system that worked for a long time. In fact if you could take the best people in the position and put them together now it would beat any system, I don't care what it is.

'However teams don't play that way now, and I doubt if they ever will again. Everyone still looks for skill in midfield but they've got to be dynamos now, and in fact the full-backs are the ones who need pace so they can overlap.'

The football career of Jack McGinn was soon relegated to playing for the office team, when he joined the circulation department of Beaverbrook Newspapers, then the Rolls-Royce of publishing houses.

He smiled as he recalled: 'I captained the team to victory in the Max Aitken trophy, which was competed for between the London, Manchester and Glasgow offices. I had to suffer such guys as Allan Herron and Bobby Maitland in the team.'

Like the Celtic chairman both progressed from the *Evening Citizen* office team and are now distinguished senior sports journalists.

However during his time in newspapers Jack McGinn nurtured the idea of a club newspaper for Celtic fans only, as he explained: 'There were and are items of interest for fans of the club, but no newspaper wants or has space to publish them because they only concern Celtic fans.

'It is also a place for the club to speak directly to their supporters on a whole range of issues, among the most vital the constant repeating of the stand against hooliganism.

'That was the idea behind it and in 1965 I met the club directors

36

for the first time to discuss it. I was told to advance it a bit further and returned for a second meeting with the project costed.

'Jock Stein was at that meeting. He had been appointed manager but had to stay with Hibs for a short spell. I got the go-ahead, and he told me to keep a space on the front page of the first issue – we would have the Scottish Cup on it.'

And that was the way it worked out when the first issue of the new paper, *The Celtic View*, was published.

Jack McGinn is immensely proud of the publishing babe he founded. 'I worked out it would take £600 to launch it and Sir Robert Kelly said if the club lost that amount it wouldn't be the end of the world.

'I don't think he meant it as a slap in the face, it was just an indication the board were not too sure the paper would get off the ground. But the following April we were able to pay back that £600 and from that day the club have never had to subsidize it, although the financial set-up was eventually re-structured so that the match programme and the newspaper became inter-dependent on each other.'

So that idea led to Jack McGinn's close connection with Celtic, and eventually to him becoming the man in charge of their commercial operations.

But a seat on the board was not something he thought about, for the simple reason he was not a shareholder. Because of the club's structure shares are not available on the open market.

'It never entered my head that I would become a director. I could have made £150 million for Celtic, and it wouldn't have made any difference if the board had decided they didn't want me. The invitation had to come from within. I was lucky enough to be made a present of some shares, and the same again when I was elected chairman.'

Jack McGinn, the first chairman for nearly eighty years not to come from the ruling Kelly and White families or to be a major shareholder such as Tom Devlin, still believes fervently that Celtic's structure as a private limited company is correct.

'I feel very strongly that whatever this club has achieved in its hundred years, it has retained its heritage or identity or whatever you like to call it, and I wouldn't like that to disappear.

'Maybe Celtic would have been twice as successful if they had become a public company earlier this century. There's no way of telling that. But by the course they did take they totally retained their identity, and I think that's something precious.

'The jersey is the same, the Irish origins are still remembered. We're not an Irish club and have never claimed to be, but we always remember that people of Irish descent had the initial idea.'

It is an impossible mission to look forward to the next 100 years but the chairman admitted: 'If in the future we found we were unable to compete in pure financial terms, it's not outside our capabilities to produce money without necessarily going public.'

Perhaps the pace of change may be swifter in the next century of the club's life than in their first, for Jack McGinn pointed out: 'In Celtic terms the changes which happened from our founding in 1888 to the middle 1950s were very, very slow.

'For much of that period football was far and away the people's sport. Most folk worked a five-and-a-half day week. They finished at lunch-time on a Saturday, and then went to a match.

'There was no TV, car-owning was relatively rare, golf was not the popular sport it is today and with thousands living in tenements even gardening was hardly an occupation of the masses.

'No team had a big travelling support. If Celtic played against Dundee at Dens Park the support came from local fans of our club. You drew people from the area where you were playing; because they didn't have TV they wanted to see their favourites in real live action.

'It also meant that many fans regularly watched Celtic Reserves in action because they couldn't travel to away matches.'

The set-up has now completely changed, with vast armies of travelling supporters following the major sides not just all over Scotland, but regarding even Europe as almost their own backyard.

Yet McGinn is a traditionalist in his defence of winter football for he firmly believes the counter-attractions of participating in summer sports, trips to the coast with kids, gardening etc, would make it difficult to draw massive crowds on a regular scale for summer soccer.

But he is not old-fashioned in his ideas for Celtic Park, which will be the venue for massive changes in the coming months. He said: 'As it is at present the inside structure of the stand is close enough to its original design of the twenties.

'There's a home and away dressing-room, a room for the referee and linesmen, a boardroom and a wee tea-room. The only real change has been that the snooker room became a table-tennis room and now is the presidential room. Never mind any cosmetic alterations that have been made, the basic structure is roughly the same.

'That has meant we have had to turn away commercial revenue. We can't have matches sponsored when we don't have the accommodation.

'People have put my arm up my back and we have had some

Celtic chairman Jack McGinn shows the new Parkhead video system, installed to help police with crowd control and spotting trouble-makers

sponsorship, but it's been done very reluctantly. I know the shortcomings of our set-up with the stand, and we almost have to put the sponsors into a hole in the corner. I don't like visitors coming and saying it's a bit of a dump. We've kept turning money away because we just didn't have the facilities.'

However a new addition to be built at the front of the stand will completely change all that. There will be space for offices, sponsors' hospitality facilities, a club exhibition and a restaurant. In short Jack McGinn's description could not be bettered: 'It will be much more civilized.'

The changes in the stand will be only one of many items in a varied programme designed to celebrate the 100 years of the club.

When we spoke, details had not been completely finalized but the chairman emphasized: 'We want to do it in a way that is a little bit special, and caters for all tastes.'

So plans have been discussed for a stage production, even a pop festival or a gala concert and a series of special dinners as well as the traditional centenary match.

'We know already many exiles are planning to return to Scotland to help us celebrate the centenary. Estimates are as high as 2000 coming from Australia alone.'

It should be a swell party for a club with one of the proudest 100 years in Scottish football!

THE LEAGUE ROLLER-COASTER

This time there was no last-day glory . . . no laps of honour for a Premier League triumph.

Instead a campaign which had begun with so much hope ended with a whimper as Celtic surrendered their title to their major rivals, Rangers.

This is not intended to re-open the wounds, hopefully bound together after the close-season break. But sometimes, with the benefit of that commodity called hindsight – what a pity they can't market it in reverse so we could look into the future – it does no harm to look back on what went wrong.

The 1986–87 season took Celtic fans on a roller-coaster. They swiftly rose to the top, and then were hurtled down in the second half of the season with only a few upbeat moments to console them as they saw Rangers move nearer their championship target.

The 44-match league programme was a marathon for players, managers, supporters and, yes, even the press. Sometimes, with games also played on a Tuesday night as well as a Wednesday night, it meant watching four major matches in one week which became too rich a soccer diet for even the most fervent enthusiast.

The addition of eight extra league games in the Premier Division, which stretched the programme to a massive 44 matches, meant fixture list planning headaches for the Scottish League. Their solution was to cram as many matches as possible into the first half of the season, when the weather is usually better. European games, internationals and Skol Cup matches had all to be fitted into a schedule which was punishing on the top teams, most of whom played with hardly a break from August to December.

The hectic programme began with no fewer than five league matches, plus two Skol Cup games, in the first month.

AUGUST: The season started with one of the happier moments, the unfurling of the Premier League flag and the presentation of the Championship trophy.

The opponents were Dundee, who fell to a Mo Johnston goal, as the little striker signalled start-of-the-season sharpness.

The determination of Brian McClair shows as he slots the ball past keeper Chris Woods to score against Rangers at Parkhead

He was back on target in the first mid-week match, the away game against Motherwell at Fir Park when he scored twice and the scoring rivalry with team-mate Brian McClair was sparked off. McClair notched two, one from a penalty, against his old club.

Clydebank are always difficult opposition for big-name teams on their own Kilbowie Park, and so it proved when Celtic made their first visit of the season when only a Johnston goal two minutes from time took Davie Hay's men to full points.

The first of a long series of duels with Aberdeen – they were to be opponents in the Skol Cup and the Scottish Cup – began with a 1–1 draw at Parkhead when the Celtic scorer was Murdo MacLeod.

Two points were lost when the 'Old Firm' made history on the last day of the month, Sunday, 31 August – the first time a league match had been televised live in Scotland involving Celtic and Rangers.

The TV companies' desire to screen such a programme had sparked off a series of events the season before which had involved talk of breakaway leagues and an eventual change in the number of Premier League clubs. This time there was no such fuss, and in view of the boring nature of much of the off-the-field row the season before many football supporters must have found it merciful that an agreement about TV had been achieved peaceably.

It was the first 'Old Firm' match involving Rangers' new signings from England, Chris Woods and Terry Butcher, and it was a happy debut for them – Rangers won 1–0 in a game in which Celtic showed very little attacking skills.

SEPTEMBER: Celtic showed more attacking appetite against one of the newly promoted sides, Hamilton, when they visited Parkhead. The score was 4–1, with a first-half hat-trick from Alan McInally and another goal from Johnston.

Dundee United are always among the hardest of opponents in any season, and so it proved when Celtic went to Tannadice. However they should have come away with better than one point, after Brian McClair and Paul McStay had given them a two-goal lead, but United fought back to make the final score 2–2.

Skol Cup and European games were sandwiched into mid-week spots, with the League confined to Saturday dates.

Celtic shrugged aside the heavy fixture list to crush Hibs 5–1 at Parkhead. Paul McStay put Celtic in the lead, but the Edinburgh side equalized to make it 1–1 at half-time. However two goals from Brian McClair, and one each from McInally and Johnston gave the final score-line a healthy look from Celtic's point of view.

Mo Johnston was making a habit of scoring late goals to give Celtic full points, and he popped up in that role against Falkirk at Brockville. Brian McClair had missed from a first-half penalty, but Johnston broke down Falkirk's well organized defence with a goal eight minutes from time.

OCTOBER: Two home games, same score-line and same scorers – that was the start of the month treat for Celtic fans as their side defeated St Mirren 2–0 at Parkhead with goals from Johnston and McClair, and then followed up with an action replay against Hearts. The goals even came in the same order, but against Hearts McClair's effort came from a penalty.

It was proving to be a grand month for Celtic supporters, as their team travelled north to crush Dundee 3–0 at Dens Park, a happier visit than later in the season. The goals all came in the

The joy of Brian McClair . . . as he celebrates that goal which meant the match ended in a 1–1 draw

Above: Celtic old boy, Roddie MacDonald, now with Hearts, tries to make sure Brian McClair is kept away from the ball at Tynecastle

Left: If you can't get the ball stop the man . . . Rangers skipper Terry Butcher seems to be putting the old motto of defenders into action against Brian McClair

second half with the old reliables scoring, two from Johnston and one from McClair.

Motherwell were next on the hit list, with a 3–1 defeat when they visited Parkhead. The scorers were McInally, two, and the other came from the very promising Tony Shepherd.

Celtic had a break from league duties for the tough programme of the European Cup match against Dynamo Kiev, followed by the Skol Cup Final against Rangers.

The disappointment of the defeat by the Ibrox side was intense, but Celtic manfully shrugged at least some of that aside with a 6–0 defeat of Clydebank at Parkhead. The goals were scored by MacLeod, McClair, two, McInally, two, and Mark McGhee.

NOVEMBER: Only six days after the controversial Skol Cup Final at Hampden the 'Old Firm' met again. As so often happens after a soccer storm this was trouble-free and Brian McClair scored for Celtic in a 1–1 draw at Parkhead.

International team-mates, club rivals . . . Mo Johnston attempts to find a
way round Aberdeen skipper Willie Miller

Toe to toe . . . Rangers' Jimmy Nichol and Celtic's Mo Johnston try to get the ball in an Old Firm game

It was strictly back to bread-and-butter business after another major Cup disappointment, the defeat by Dynamo Kiev in the European Cup. There can be few greater contrasts than the giant stadium in the Ukraine, and homely Douglas Park. Almost inevitably the scorers were McClair, from a penalty, and Johnston, in a 2–1 victory over Hamilton.

Celtic were at their most commanding of the entire season at this stage in the league and they proved it with yet another goal in the final stages of a match from Johnston. That goal, nine minutes from time, dumped Dundee United at Parkhead and kept Celtic clear of the pack at the top of the Premier Division.

Hibs were the next to fall, as a second-half goal from McClair dumped them 1–0 at Easter Road.

Back to Parkhead in a busy month for matches, and Falkirk were beaten 4–2 with goals from Johnston with a double, McInally and Peter Grant. It was a harder fought victory than the score indicates, for at one stage Falkirk equalized . . . but the victory put Celtic a massive EIGHT points ahead of Rangers.

There were still two games to go in a seven-match league schedule for the month. An away game against Aberdeen, postponed because of the Skol Cup Final, was squeezed in and new Aberdeen manager Ian Porterfield saw his side draw 1–1 with Celtic, when Brian McClair scored from a penalty. It was an incredible spot-kick story, for McClair missed with his first effort and in the resultant scramble a second penalty was awarded for the Celtic expert to score.

Celtic then travelled to Love Street, and finished off a satisfactory month with a 1–0 victory, the scorer was defender Pierce O'Leary.

By now Celtic were seven points clear of second-placed Dundee United, and an amazing NINE points in front of Rangers, who had played a game less.

DECEMBER: The first cracks appeared as Celtic went to Tynecastle for a mid-week visit to Hearts. The crowds were so large the kick-off had to be delayed. But there was no joy in the result for the army of Celtic fans. It was the half-way mark in the league programme, and a Neil Berry goal gave Hearts a 1–0 victory.

Still, the set-back did not at the time seem too severe. It was only Celtic's second defeat in the 22 games which made up the first half of their Premier League programme.

They were back on the rails by the Saturday, with a sharp double by Mo Johnston dumping Dundee 2–0 in the second half at Parkhead.

48   *Opposite*: A friendly Bear . . . skipper Roy Aitken is for once at peace on a football field at the club's pre-season picture session

Above: The strain game . . . as former Celtic manager Davie Hay (*right*) and his chief coach, Tommy Craig, watch a match from the Parkhead dug-out

Below: The winner is McInally . . . as Dundee United's Jim and Alan of Celtic from the clan of McInally joust for the ball in a league match at Parkhead

Right: First to the ball . . . Paul McGugan shrugs off a challenge from Dundee United's Kevin Gallacher

The power and the promise of one of Scotland's brightest young defenders . . . Celtic's Derek Whyte races clear in a match against Dundee United

Going for goal . . . Mo Johnston in the role that has upset so many defences

Above: Scotland's most dangerous striker last season, Brian McClair, takes on the Dundee defence at Parkhead

Below left: The perfect balance of one of Scotland's most skilful players, as Paul McStay moves to set up another Celtic attack

Below right: Boss of the penalty area . . . and keeper Pat Bonner tells his defensive mates how it should be done

Above: New Year mudlarks . . . as Celtic's Pat Bonner dives to smother the ball at Ibrox watched by (*left to right*), Paul McGugan (Celtic), Terry Butcher (Rangers), Brian McClair (Celtic), Graham Roberts (Rangers) and Roy Aitken (Celtic)

Below left: We've made it . . . and scorer Tommy Burns salutes the crowd as Mo Johnston congratulates him after his winning penalty in the Skol Cup semi-final against Motherwell

Below right: The man who caused so much terror to Scotland's defenders last season, Brian McClair, heads for goal

Up for the Cup . . . as (*left to right*) Celtic's Derek Whyte, Alan McInally and Roy Aitken guard Rangers skipper Terry Butcher in the Skol Cup Final with Parkhead youngster Tony Shepperd looking on

Man on the move . . . Paul McStay works hard in midfield to get his attack going against Dundee United

However a string of draws, with the same score-line in three successive games, meant the year ended on a note of uncertainty.

The dismal series of results began against Motherwell at Fir Park, when Brian McClair gave Celtic the lead just on half-time, but immediately after the interval the home side equalized and the final score was 1–1.

A draw against Aberdeen is hardly a disaster, and at Parkhead an Alan McInally goal gave a repeat score, 1–1, of the match at Pittodrie the previous month.

However two days after Christmas the 1–1 score against Clydebank at Kilbowie must put Celtic into the Santa Claus category. Even allowing for the fact that Clydebank inevitably raise their game on their own ground against the top teams, Celtic should not have recorded such a result against a team who were eventually to be relegated. McClair was the scorer of the goal which won a point.

JANUARY: An ever harsher wind blew a chill New Year entry into 1987 for Celtic, with a game which captured in essence the battle for Premier League supremacy between the 'Old Firm'.

Rangers won 2–0 at Ibrox in the traditional Ne'erday derby game. It was not so much the score-line that brought frowns to the Celtic supporters, although it hardly made for a joyful start to the year, but it was the manner of the defeat.

Rarely can the Ibrox side have looked so far ahead, for Celtic's attacking flair never showed itself, apart from one powerful Paul McStay shot saved by keeper Chris Woods.

However, as if to make up for the stuttering shows of the previous week Celtic really turned on the attacking power against Hamilton at Parkhead finishing 8–3 winners. The goal parade was headed by Brian McClair with an amazing four, and the others were divided two each by Murdo MacLeod and McInally.

But even in victory there was evidence of the shadows which persisted over the Celtic side, two late goals carelessly conceded to take an edge off the win.

There was much tougher opposition in the next game, and another two points were lost when Celtic were beaten 3–2 by Dundee United at Tannadice. Yet at one stage it seemed as if Celtic would sweep to a marvellous victory when, with two McClair goals, they fought back to 2–2 only to be beaten by a late Eamonn Bannon goal for United.

A narrow, but welcome, victory against Hibs at Parkhead followed that reversal, when Anton Rogan marked his recent introduction to the league team with his first goal for a 1–0 win.

There was another hard-fought victory at Brockville, where

Opposite: Rambo rules . . . Alan McInally takes on the Dundee United defence at Parkhead

The passion of an Old Firm game, as Roy Aitken lectures Rangers' Derek Ferguson after a free-kick award to the Celtic skipper

Falkirk took the lead but two goals by Johnston gave Celtic a 2–1 victory.

FEBRUARY: A flying start to the month with a 3–0 win against St Mirren, and a sprightly showing on the wing by Mark Smith. The scorers at home were Johnston, two, and McClair.

But the hiccups continued with a 1–1 draw against Hearts at Parkhead; the two teams were to meet again the following Saturday in the Scottish Cup at Tynecastle. Brian McClair was

Three to one for Celtic . . . as Dundee United's Dave Bowman takes on
Mo Johnston (half hidden), Murdo MacLeod and Mark McGhee

the scorer of an early goal which gave Celtic the lead, but Hearts equalized late in the game.

Significantly the lead over Rangers had been cut to one point.

The month ended with the greatest single disaster of the entire season, a 4–1 defeat from Dundee at Dens Park. Dundee had not taken a point or scored a goal against Celtic in three matches before this game. It seemed they would not improve on their record when McClair gave the Parkhead side a 1–0 interval lead. But the roof simply fell in during the second half as the Dens Park side banged in four goals to finish as deserved winners.

MARCH: It was always going to be uphill in the league race after that, but Celtic tried manfully to stage a revival with a 3–1 victory at home against Motherwell.

This was the first game after Johnston had announced he did not intend to sign his new contract, and a large section of the crowd let the striker know what they thought of his decision.

The scorers were Roy Aitken, Tom McAdam with an own goal, and Tony Shepherd.

No joy at Pittodrie, where Celtic were beaten 1–0 by Aberdeen, but McInally and a double by McClair, one from a penalty, gave a 3–0 victory against Clydebank at Parkhead.

An uninspired 3–2 victory against relegation-doomed Hamilton was achieved at Douglas Park, thanks to goals from McInally, McClair and Archdeacon.

APRIL: But all the worries of the second half of the season were swept aside for 90 minutes the following week, when Celtic notched a comprehensive 3–1 victory over Rangers at Parkhead.

It was their first win against the Ibrox men since Graeme Souness had taken over as manager, and it was in complete contrast to the last league match at Ibrox.

Brian McClair set up the win with two first-half penalties, rightly awarded despite Rangers disputing the second award. Rangers pulled one goal back, but Celtic sealed victory late in the match when Ibrox keeper Chris Woods and Jimmy Nicholl messed up a pass-back and Owen Archdeacon nipped in to score a third goal.

Celtic made a valiant attempt to keep the championship alive with a 4–1 victory against Hibs at Easter Road, even though they conceded the first goal. The scorers were McInally, Johnston, McStay and McClair.

But there was another set-back the next week when Dundee United equalized a Brian McClair goal in the final stage of the game at Parkhead to make it 1–1.

Celtic then notched a 3–1 victory against Cup finalists, soon to

It's a Murdo MacLeod dance, as he tries to get the ball past Dundee United's Eamonn Bannon

Rambo in full flight . . . as Alan McInally tries to beat the Dundee United defensive barrier of John Clark and keeper Billy Thomson

be crowned Cup winners, St Mirren. The goals came from McClair, two, and Johnston, in the final flourish of their partnership.

MAY: It all ended not with a bang, but a whimper. Celtic trailed against Falkirk at Parkhead right from the start, equalized with a controversial McClair penalty, and then lost out in the closing minutes to a winning goal from self-confessed Celtic fan Jimmy Gilmour to go down 2–1.

In the far north at Pittodrie a 1–1 draw was enough to clinch the title for Rangers.

The next week was merely the second stage of the anti-climax stakes, when a penalty by John Robertson gave Hearts a 1–0 victory at Tynecastle.

The contrast with the final game of the previous season, when the championship had been clinched at Paisley, could not have been greater.

MY EUROPEAN DREAM
by Paul McStay

Paul McStay has a collection of silverware which any top-class jeweller might envy for display in his window. Scotland's major domestic honours – Premier League, Scottish Cup and League Cup – have all come his way, and at the age of 23 he has more winners' medals than many players collect in a lifetime.

He also made his mark at international level with Scotland in a string of successful sides from the Schoolboys team through the ranks of the Under-16 professional youth team, then advancing to Under-17, Under-19, Under-21 and finally the full team.

The list is glittering, and apparently endless. But Paul admits there is one gap which so far he and his team-mates have failed to fill. Unlike the Celtic teams of the late sixties and early seventies, the present squad have been unable to advance beyond the early rounds of European competition.

Paul admitted: 'It's marvellous to qualify for Europe, a great bonus every season and we all look forward to it. But really it's a disappointment to us all not to have had a sustained run in these tournaments like the club had not so long ago.

'I thought it was going to start against Dynamo Kiev because we came so close in Russia.

'Europe must be our top priority. I think success builds on success and it spreads right through the club. Look at Dundee United in the UEFA Cup.'

Still, at only 23 there is surely time for this young man with one of the most famous of Celtic names, to take part in that revival of the side's fortunes in Europe which is his aim.

His great-uncles were the legendary Celtic players, Willie and Jimmy McStay, stalwart figures of the twenties and thirties. The name McStay is indelibly linked with Celtic, and the Scottish Cup!

The family ties go back more than sixty years when Willie and Jimmy McStay appeared in the 1923 Final – a match Celtic won 1-0 against Hibs.

Willie and Jimmy played together in five finals for Celtic, winning three and losing twice. Willie's last final was the 4–0

55

Above: The shooting power of Paul McStay . . . as he unleashes an effort against Clydebank

Right: Higher and higher, but not high enough for Paul McStay as Hibs' Gordon Chisholm outjumps him

defeat in 1928 by Rangers, but Jimmy went on to win two more medals in 1931 and 1933.

Willie was capped 13 times for Scotland, and Jimmy became one of only six Celtic managers, slotting in after Willie Maley and before Jimmy McGrory who was followed by Jock Stein, Billy McNeill, Davie Hay then McNeill again.

Under Davie Hay both Paul and his elder brother Willie played in two Cup Finals, losing in 1984 and winning in 1985. That equalled the record of the Callaghan brothers, Willie and Tom, who twice played in Cup Finals, losing in 1965 and winning in 1968.

Surely the torch has been successfully passed on, for Paul showed his talent early on. The boy from Larkhall was even given

a trial by Leeds United when he was only 12. He went south accompanied by his brother Willie, and Colin Walsh, who later moved to Nottingham Forest and then Charlton Athletic.

However there was really only one club he wanted to play for, and Jock Stein moved quickly to snap the lad up on an 'S' form. It was surely one of the best legacies the Big Man left to his managerial successors at Parkhead.

Paul had given an early glimpse of his potential in a televized victory for Scotland's Under-15 schoolboys who won 5–4 against England at Wembley. The talents of Paul McStay developed so swiftly that there was no way he could be kept out the first team, even though he was only 17.

He got a swift early lesson in the way football can raise a team up, and kick them down again just as quickly. Paul made his debut before only 11,281 fans in a Scottish Cup tie at Parkhead against Queen of the South in January 1982. There was no problem in overcoming the opposition from a lower division, Celtic won 4–0 and a rare name among the goal-scorers was skipper Danny McGrain.

However only a few weeks later Celtic's hopes of Cup success came to an abrupt end, and this time there was a very different atmosphere. For in a packed Pittodrie, with a capacity 24,000 crowd, a John Hewitt goal for Aberdeen took them through one of the key ties of the season.

Paul said: 'I found the pace tremendous. It was such a change from what I had been used to before then.'

Happily for the youngster he was in the Celtic team when they returned to Pittodrie a week later, this time for a Premier League fixture. And it was a different score-line, with Celtic winning 3–1 – the third goal was scored by Master Paul McStay.

He played in seven league matches, followed by a spell of sitting on the bench as a substitute until the last match of the season. That was a 3–0 victory for Celtic against St Mirren at Parkhead which earned them the Premier League Championship and won a winner's medal for the talented teenager.

The career of Paul McStay was off and running!

He has also made an impression as an international player, groomed by playing in the team which won the European youth championship and then a year later competed in the World Finals in Mexico.

It led to his debut at full international level against Uruguay in 1983 when he played in a Scotland team which defeated the South Americans 2–0 at Hampden. This was not to be his last encounter with the international squad of that nation!

International manager Jock Stein, rarely given to public praise

Hands together . . . as Brian McClair and Paul McStay move to get a defensive wall together watched by referee Yeats during a game against Hearts

of youngsters, described it as the most impressive international debut he had ever seen. No player could expect higher praise than that!

Just over a year later he was in the Scotland team which started out on a road that was to prove very long to reach Mexico, and the 1986 World Cup Finals.

He scored twice in the 3–0 defeat of Iceland in the opening match of the qualifying programme, and again the praise was pouring in his direction. This time it came from Luis Suarez, who

The battle of the Young Ones . . . Rangers' Derek Ferguson and Paul McStay have a tussle for the ball in an Old Firm game

once graced the strips of Barcelona and Inter Milan as one of the best post-war forwards in Europe. He was, by 1984, the right hand man of Spanish team boss Miguel Munoz, weighing up in advance all their international opponents at senior and Under-21 levels.

After McStay's double – his first-ever international goals – Suarez said: 'That young man played so very well. I have watched Scotland a lot recently, and there is no limit to what he can achieve. I have been greatly impressed by his progress.'

A month later Paul was in the Scotland side which defeated Spain 3–1 at Hampden, and the Celtic connection was maintained when two of the goals were scored by Mo Johnston, and the other by former Celt, Kenny Dalglish to produce an unforgettable half. It was perhaps the finest match of Jock Stein's managership of the Scotland team.

Spain got their revenge in the return match, a 1–0 controversial game in Seville, which was followed by the display Stein himself regarded as the worst in his time as manager. That was the 1–0 defeat by Wales at Hampden, which meant such an uphill battle for Scotland.

Paul McStay was not brought back into the side until the very last match which ensured Scotland would have a place in Mexico.

That was when they drew 0–0 with Australia in Melbourne, and this time there was a different manager with Alex Ferguson taking over from Jock Stein, who had died tragically at the end of the second game against Wales, played at Ninian Park, Cardiff.

Paul was part of the squad who travelled to Mexico, his second visit to that country with all its additional problems of playing at altitude. This time he was prepared for the TV cameras and the media circus which reported on the World Cup. It had been different when the youth team arrived. They were all most bemused that when they flew into Mexico City airport it had been shown on live TV.

McStay played in only one match, the controversy-studded final game for Scotland, when they drew 0–0 with Uruguay. They needed a victory to carry them through to the second stage of the Finals for the first time in their history.

There had been controversy even before the match, when manager Alex Ferguson dropped the Scotland skipper Graeme Souness and replaced him with Paul McStay. But it was nothing to the furore in the first minute of the match when the French referee sent off Uruguyan player Jose Batista for a vicious foul on Gordon Strachan.

Paul says: 'The referee would have needed to have eyes in the back of his head to have spotted everything that went on during

Above: The skill of Paul McStay, this time wearing a Scotland international jersey

Left: The battle of the Young Ones . . . Paul McStay flies past Aberdeen's teenage defender David Robertson

that match. It was unbelievable. The Uruguyans were up to every dirty trick in the book, and a few more I didn't know had been invented. I don't know if the fans back home saw it all on TV, for sometimes even the cameras can miss some of the incidents.

'Believe me, it wasn't pleasant. It was to Scotland's credit that day we didn't get involved. I suppose it was one of the biggest disappointments of my career. You dream of playing in the World Cup Finals, and then it turned into a game like that. I felt cheated.'

The McStay family fortunes of the current clan have fluctuated. Last season brother Willie was transferred to Huddersfield. Paul is likely to be in the spotlight when his own contract expires at the end of this coming season, and there will inevitably be more talk about a move abroad. He was once reported to be the subject of a £2 million bid by Inter Milan.

But Paul treats all the speculation like that with the same cool attitude he brings to his play on the park. He said: 'Obviously I've thought about it. I suppose you always wonder how you would do over there on the Continent.

'But really it's not something that concerns me every day. I'm getting married next spring and it would be a big decision to start our life abroad.

'I'll just wait and take it as it comes.'

At the moment he is content in his Lanarkshire home of Larkhall, always recognized as one of the strongholds of Rangers fans but he says: 'Our neighbours are brilliant. We couldn't ask for any better.'

Despite his super-cool image on the park, Paul does admit to a few butterflies before big games. 'They make me nervous, but I'm all right once I get on the park.'

And he's been known to sit up and watch videos until 3 a.m. in the morning to unwind after particularly gruelling mid-week games.

However that does not diminish his appetite for the game. Many players have complained about the length of the stretched out programme of 44 league games but Paul simply says: 'I've found it enjoyable. The season passed really quickly. We had so many mid-week games that we did a lot more light training to let us concentrate on matches.'

The only disappointment was that at the end of the marathon slog there were no trophies in the Parkhead trophy cabinet to show for it.

The determination of Paul McStay, this time playing for his club

CUP HEARTBREAKS

Cup success and Celtic have gone together for nearly a century. But sadly for the Parkhead club and their legions of fans, hopes for more Cups to decorate their trophy cases in the year of their centenary were dashed in three tournaments – the Skol Cup, the European Champions Cup and the Scottish Cup.

However before Celtic were eliminated, each competition provided a fascinating mixture of excitement and controversy which made them memorable, if not always for the right reasons.

Controversy raged even before the first round of the *European Cup*, in which Celtic were drawn against the League of Ireland champions, Shamrock Rovers.

The trouble was that the Milltown ground in Dublin had a capacity of only 22,000, limited for the game to 18,000. And there were still fears about safety because the League of Ireland club had to erect a temporary stand and terracing.

Celtic Supporters Association secretary George Delaney expressed his fears about the venue when he said, 'The SFA should ask UEFA to make sure the ground is up to standard, with enough proper exits and entrances.'

In the event, perhaps with a bit of the luck of the Irish, the crowd were all shoe-horned successfully into the ground and the match passed off without incident.

Celtic achieved their mission of winning and scoring away from home, when Murdo MacLeod gave them a valuable first-leg lead eight minutes from time. But, with commendable honesty, manager Davie Hay said, 'We were lucky to get a goal. A draw would have been a fairer result.'

The furore before the second leg was intense, sparked off by Mo Johnston's newspaper articles claiming he would be happy to play for Manchester United.

The mock battle before the real thing . . . Celtic's Roy Aitken and Jimmy Nichol of Rangers have a friendly sparring session at a sponsor's photo-session before the Skol Cup Final

The delight of a Cup Final place, shown in the faces of Mo Johnston and Tommy Burns after Tommy's penalty-kick winner against Motherwell in the Skol Cup semi-final

However if the fans were talking before the game about his off-the-field statements they were soon talking about what he was doing on the pitch, for Mo scored two goals to take Celtic comfortably through to the second round on a 3–0 aggregate.

And it seemed Celtic could not escape the headlines, for when the second-round draw was made the Scottish champions were drawn against Russian aces, Dynamo Kiev. Immediately fears were expressed about travelling to the Russian city only 60 miles from Chernobyl where the previous spring a nuclear reactor had been involved in a major disaster, devastating the countryside around with radioactive dust. The Foreign Office had advised that no one should travel there, unless it was absolutely necessary.

Celtic's new chairman Jack McGinn said, 'We are very concerned. We have young men with families in our team and we don't want to expose them to any possible risks.'

Skipper Roy Aitken added, 'If there's any danger to health then we should keep well clear of Kiev.'

Sensibly the club made a thorough check on the radiation dangers in Kiev before they decided to go ahead with the tie. Said

The lethal finishing power of Brian McClair, shown as the striker darts to the left of the six-yards area to head Celtic's first goal against Motherwell in the Skol Cup semi-final

The lethal finishing power of Roy Aitken, who leaves Motherwell keeper John Gardiner stranded to score Celtic's second Skol Cup semi-final goal

chairman McGinn after a week of checks on the situation, 'If I thought there was any danger to Celtic players we would not be going. For that matter I wouldn't want to be there myself.

'Our doctor has made exhaustive checks, and we are now confident there is no danger. In fact we may be safer in Kiev than in other Russian cities because of the precautions which have been taken there.'

But first the Russian champions – winners of the European Cup Winners' Cup the previous season – had to play in Scotland.

Their hotel in Glasgow flew the Red Flag in their honour, and club officials staggered staff with requests for a five-course lunch, and a seven-course dinner. They also requested special videos for the players, and specified they had to be without violence but have enough action to overcome the language difficulties. A member of the hotel staff joked, 'Maybe we should show them Donald Duck.'

The Russians were among the most formidable opposition Celtic could have faced. The bulk of their team were internationals from their country's World Cup squad in Mexico the previous summer.

However the atmosphere before the game was completely friendly. The teams exchanged videos of their last league matches to help the two managers plot each other's downfall. Manager Davie Hay gave pre-match instructions to his club's fans as well as his players. 'Other managers talk about patience from the crowd. But we'll have a go. I don't want patience from anyone.'

Six internationals lined up in the Kiev side, but it was Celtic who almost took the lead in just five minutes when Johnston headed down and from six yards out Alan McInally belted it against the junction of the post and the bar.

However Dynamo took the lead in 17 minutes when Vadim Yevtushenko scored, and it was the first of two hammer-blows for Celtic. Three minutes later a disgraceful tackle by Alexander Zavarov removed Tommy Burns from the action. . . and put him out of football for months to come. The Russians, normally so correct, were lucky not to be reduced to ten men for such an attack.

Celtic were desperately anxious to do well in front of the 47,858 fans who roared them on and with only eleven minutes left they got some reward for their industry and effort. Murdo MacLeod, trying to set up yet another Celtic attack, sent the ball into the penalty area where Johnston hit it first against keeper Viktor Chanov but then managed to force the rebound into the net.

Obviously Celtic now faced an uphill task to save the tie, because the Russians had achieved one of the main aims of any team in Europe – to score a goal away from home.

Still, their preparations for the return game were meticulous

Battle honours – Roy Aitken, suffering from a nasty head wound, receives his Skol Cup semi-final man-of-the-match award from Alloa Breweries Sales representative, Ken Ralston

and nowhere more so than in the food department. Celtic took their own food with them. Broth, vegetables, tea, coffee, meat and bread were put into special hampers along with ten gallons of drinking water. Tim Kelly, then manager of the Grosvenor Hotel in Glasgow, was in charge of the preparations and the dishes were frozen after they were cooked.

71

However it was not food but players which was Celtic's major worry for the second game, played before 100,000 fans in Kiev. Skipper Roy Aitken was suffering from flu, and Alan McInally felt ill on the flight.

SFA secretary Ernie Walker was a guest of Celtic to act as an observer; however the Russians were attentive hosts.

In the event, Aitken was able to lend his towering presence to a cause which seemed totally beyond Celtic when veteran international star Oleg Blokhin scored in just 12 minutes to put Kiev ahead on aggregate.

Spirits drooped back home as fans listened to the radio commentary and then were revived magically four minutes into the second half when Mark McGhee made it 1–1 on the night, and only 2–1 on aggregate. Sadly defensive mistakes let Yacovenko and then Yevtushenko score in 72 minutes and the final minute of the game.

The last gasp goal gave an almost unbalanced score-line in the Russians favour of 3–1 in the second leg and 4–2 on aggregate.

It was the sixth successive season that Celtic had failed to make the last eight in Europe, but this time against virtually the Soviet national side. There was disappointment but no disgrace in losing to such powerful opponents.

The European Cup and the *Skol Cup* are almost intertwined on the soccer fixture calendar, but the controversy of the first competition was a mere molehill compared to the mountain which erupted like a football volcano over the second.

The tournament, again seeded, started quietly enough for Celtic with two victories against First Division opposition. Airdrie were the first team to be swept out of the way, with a 2–0 victory at Parkhead when the scorer was Brian McClair with two goals. They went one better against Dumbarton, again at Parkhead, when the score was 3–0, and the men who found the net were Johnston with two and one from McStay.

But the fireworks were soon to explode, and the action began at Pittodrie in a quarter-final battle of the giants against Aberdeen.

Extra time and then penalties were scheduled if the match was still even at the end of the first 90 minutes. The safety net of a two-legged quarter-final, or a replay, had been swept away in the Scottish League's understandable anxiety to work their way through as much of the heavy domestic programme as possible before the onset of any bad weather.

There were certainly enough incidents to keep the capacity Pittodrie crowd roaring their way through a cup-tie drenched with excitement.

Aberdeen scored first, through Robert Connor, in just 13

The joy of a Cup goal, as Mo Johnston embraces scorer Brian McClair
after Celtic's first score in the Skol Cup semi-final

The rakes' progress . . . as Mo Johnston, Alan McInally and Brian McClair line up as Celtic's strike force before the European Cup match against Dynamo Kiev

minutes but Celtic plugged away and in 67 minutes Mo Johnston scored when he hit home a Paul McStay cross at the second attempt.

Four minutes later Celtic were in desperate trouble when sub Tony Shepherd was sent off for a foul on Steve Gray – the Parkhead youngster had already been booked.

However Celtic, down to ten men, pushed the game to extra time although they were further handicapped when defender Derek Whyte had to go off injured, and was replaced by Owen Archdeacon. The teams were still locked at 1–1 after two hours, and the game moved to a penalty decider.

Skipper Roy Aitken saw his effort saved by Jim Leighton, and Jim Bett scored to put Aberdeen ahead. Mo Johnston was the next to be successful, but John Hewitt had his shot saved by Pat Bonner. So the scores were tied at 1–1 on spot-kicks, and Peter Grant for Celtic and Peter Weir for Aberdeen made it 2–2.

However after Owen Archdeacon scored a third for Celtic the Pittodrie skipper Willie Miller missed, and Brian McClair finished it off in Celtic's favour for a 4–2 penalty score-line.

Apart from the Shepherd sending-off there were six bookings, all of which did not please Celtic manager Davie Hay who announced afterwards he did not want referee Bob Valentine to be in charge of any more of his club's matches.

Amazingly it needed another penalty-kick decider to settle the semi-final, when Celtic played Motherwell at Hampden.

The Parkhead men moved into the lead in 38 minutes when Murdo MacLeod sent Willie McStay clear and his cross was headed in against his old team by Brian McClair.

Celtic's path to the final seemed completely clear when in 60 minutes skipper Aitken scored one of the most exciting individual goals of the season, slotting the ball into the net from an acute angle after a great run from his own half and a quick 1–2 with Johnston.

However Celtic surrendered that two goal lead with defensive lapses which let Andy Walker score in 70 minutes and Paul Smith grab the equaliser two minutes from time.

After the regulation 30 minutes of extra time it was back to penalties, and this time Celtic's winning margin was closer than at Pittodrie.

Tom Boyd and Andy Walker scored for Motherwell, and Brian McClair and Mo Johnston for Celtic. John Philliben then missed for the Fir Park side, Derek Whyte and Paul McStay netted for the Parkhead men, and Brian Wright and Steve Kirk for Motherwell. So it was all down to Tommy Burns, with the tenth penalty of the shoot-out, to clinch victory for Celtic by 5–4.

The skipper charges . . . Roy Aitken prepares to sweep past Kiev's Oleg Kuznetzov

The first major Cup final clash between Celtic and the new-look, Graeme Souness-managed Rangers sparked off incredible interest. There was a 75,000 Sunday sell-out at Hampden on 26 October, with the game televised live to sixteen countries which generated more than £500,000 to make it the richest-ever final.

Sadly it was the whiff of controversy which lingered long after the game was over for which the match will be remembered. The crime count at the end was of monumental proportions. There were yellow cards for Aitken, McInally, Johnston, Whyte, Grant, Bonner and Archdeacon of Celtic, and Nicholl, McCoist and Munro of Rangers plus a red card for Johnston.

The goals, which made the final score-line 2–1 in favour of Rangers, all came in the second half. Iain Durrant put the Ibrox men ahead in 62 minutes when he scored his second goal in successive Old Firm matches. Then Celtic equalised with a goal which was worthy of any Cup final. The move was begun by Aitken, and Johnston played his part with a touch on to McClair who blasted a shot from 16 yards into the net.

But in 84 minutes Celtic, who had been the better team, suffered a body-blow decision from referee Davie Syme when he awarded a penalty kick after Aitken and Rangers skipper Terry Butcher had clashed in the box, and Davie Cooper made no mistake with the award.

Then, in the last minute of this torrid match, came football's version of the big bang! It was sparked off when stand-side linesman Arthur Wilson flagged to attract referee Syme's attention when Ally McCoist of Rangers was being yellow-carded. Rangers defender Stuart Munro and Mo Johnston were called over and the Ibrox player booked and the Celtic striker, who had earlier been yellow-carded, sent off. Johnston crossed himself as he was sent off, even though Celtic players had been instructed not to make such signs.

However it was then that referee Syme made what I regard as his biggest mistake when he sent off Tony Shepherd in error and then changed his mind. It's the first time in a Hampden final such a decision has ever been altered.

Mr Syme was trying to stop a mêlée involving protesting Celtic players when he felt a crack on the back of his head. He had just spoken to Shepherd and assumed wrongly that he had been struck by him. However as Celtic manager Davie Hay raced to the touch-line to try to calm down his players, the linesman pointed to a 50p piece on the grass to indicate to the referee that he had been hit by a coin from the enclosure.

Yet under SFA rules, with no right of appeal for orderings-off,

Shepherd would have a sending-off counting against him on his disciplinary record if the referee did not alter his decision.

The after-match press conference was as tense as the game and manager Hay did not pull back when he said pointedly:

'If it was up to me our application to join the English League would be made tomorrow. It's not sour grapes. Rangers have won the Cup and the best of luck to them. But it always seems to be the case that when we play top teams there are controversial decisions against Celtic.

'I don't know what happened with Tony Shepherd. The referee gave no explanation. You'll have to ask him. He showed the player the red card yet he finished up still playing. He changed his decision, and normally that doesn't happen. I keep getting told at the SFA the referee is always right.'

The fall-out from the Hampden clash continued the next day when the Celtic chairman, Jack McGinn, issued a statement on behalf of the board:

'Some aspects of the Skol Cup Final left us feeling rather aggrieved, but there is nothing to be gained by going over them in detail. People who saw the game live or watched it on television know the reasons for our dismay.

'Some Celtic players allowed their emotions to get the better of them, particularly in the closing moments of the game and that is an area the club will deal with internally and privately.'

The Celtic directors also praised their supporters for 'their fantastic and exemplary conduct'.

The final unhappy postscript to the bombshell match was written nearly a month later, when the SFA held their official probe into the match.

Again the Celtic supporters were given a pat on the back when SFA secretary Ernie Walker said, 'The Disciplinary Committee told the Celtic representatives it was their opinion that only the strong sense of restraint by supporters prevented a major disturbance at the ground.'

But the Parkhead players were rapped when Walker said, 'The supporters had been subjected to provocation by the behaviour of many of the club's representatives.'

Celtic were fined £5,000 for the conduct of their players, and manager Hay, after facing two committees on separate charges, was fined £600 – £250 by the Disciplinary Committee for an incident with referee Don McVicar at the end of a 2–2 draw against Dundee United at Tannadice; and £350 for making 'critical comments' about referee Syme's handling of the match against Rangers. The Celtic boss was also warned about repeating his criticism of referees.

Happy as sandboys . . . Brian McClair and Murdo MacLeod rush to
congratulate team-mate Alan McInally after his Scottish Cup goal
against Aberdeen at Pittodrie

The fine on Celtic was similar to the penalty imposed on
Rangers after the punch-up during their opening match of the
season against Hibs at Easter Road.

The SFA stated at that investigation that the fine had been
imposed because Rangers had appeared before them three times
in the previous two seasons. Celtic had not been in bother with the
SFA since the 1980 Scottish Cup Final riot when both Old Firm
clubs were fined £20,000 each.

Celtic played enough matches in the *Scottish Cup* to have
reached the final, but only succeeded in making the fourth round
of the tourney.

When the draw for the third round of the competition – the one
in which the Premier League clubs are included – was made live
on TV the best was kept to the last. Cup holders Aberdeen were
drawn against League Champions Celtic at Pittodrie.

Such was the intense demand that, for the first time ever outside
the Cup final itself, a Cup match was screened live on TV, with the
game switched to a Sunday afternoon slot.

It was a weekend in which some games were postponed, and
many questioned whether Pittodrie should have been passed

European expert Paul McStay tries to find a way round Dynamo Kiev's Pavel Yerenchuk

playable, for the pitch was caught in the frosty grip of winter. Celtic manager Davie Hay certainly had no doubts that it was not playable, a view he expressed at the end of the pulsating 2–2 draw. But he also added, 'Both sets of players deserve credit for performing as they did in conditions where serious injury was a very real prospect.'

The Parkhead challengers had taken a 2–0 half-time lead, with goals by Alan McInally and a penalty by Brian McClair. However Aberdeen fought back, watched by their former manager Alex Ferguson, by that time with Manchester United, Liverpool boss Kenny Dalglish and Billy McNeill, then with Aston Villa.

They scored twice, with goals from Jim Bett, via a penalty, and sub John Hewitt.

A massive crowd of 55,405 watched the teams return a tense no-scoring draw after extra time in the replay, and the tie was pushed to a third match. The teams could not agree on a venue – Parkhead, Pittodrie and Hampden were all suggested – and the SFA finally ruled it had to be played at Dens Park. The result, a 1–0 victory for Celtic, kept alive a proud Parkhead record. They had never lost a second Scottish Cup replay in their 99-year history.

The decisive goal came from Brian McClair in just 16 minutes and manager Hay said later, 'Not a lot separated the teams yet again. It was a marvellous tie.

'We were the better and hungrier side in the first half, but Aberdeen came back at us and we had to defend really well.'

It was the first defeat Aberdeen had experienced in 17 games since their new manager Ian Porterfield took over at Pittodrie and he praised Celtic when he said, 'They were the hungrier side. They had more players prepared to push themselves through the pain barrier to win.'

But the legacy of the punishing three matches against Aberdeen could not be judged properly that night. The truth was that both teams had slogged themselves almost to a standstill. It certainly showed when Celtic faced their next opponents, the previous season's defeated finalists, Hearts, at Tynecastle.

The match had a later kick-off to help avoid crowd congestion in Edinburgh with the capital also housing the Scotland v. Ireland rugby international at Murrayfield. And it seemed destined for yet another replay. Hearts, like Celtic, had taken three matches in the previous round to win through against First Division Kilmarnock. Then ten minutes from time John Robertson scored with a superb free-kick, and Hearts had beaten Celtic in the Cup for the first time since the 1956 final.

MEMORIES ARE MADE OF THIS

A lone figure running round Parkhead to the cheering adulation of thousands of Celtic fans packed on the terracings. . . . A warm evening in Lisbon as a sea of green and white supporters run on to the National Stadium to hail the first-ever British victory in the European Cup. Twenty years separate these events, yet there is a soccer thread that connects them over the two decades.

The man alone in the spotlight was Roy Aitken, the tall, craggy-faced Celtic skipper who typifies the special pride in the jersey which has always marked the great Parkhead players. The event in Lisbon was the winning of the European Cup in May 1967, just two months short of twenty years before Roy Aitken took that very special bow at his testimonial match against Manchester United at Parkhead.

The fans were paying tribute, in one case to an individual, in the other to a team, who had surely achieved something special and in so doing brought honour to the club they loved.

Let us first look back at the Lisbon Lions. In the previous book in this series I spotlighted the fact that 1987 was the twentieth anniversary of the 2–1 Celtic victory against Inter Milan in the final of the European Cup.

The Lisbon Lions' marvellous achievement has always been categorized as a never-to-be-forgotten event . . . but surely not even the class of 1967 who graduated with the highest honours in club football could ever have imagined just how much it would be remembered. The outpourings in newspapers, television and radio around the time of that magical 25 May date were quite fantastic.

I was fortunate to be a guest at a special lunch organized by my newspaper, the *Daily Record*, to celebrate that European Cup Final victory. I don't remember laughing as much for years. The men of Lisbon didn't just meander down memory lane, they went back over the years at motorway speed. It seemed twenty years just vanished, and the stories and the jokes were as fresh as if they had been newly minted. As my colleague Alex Cameron wrote: 'What astounded me about this rare get-together of sporting greats was

Cup time! Roy Aitken's wife, Jane, is the centre of attraction as she holds the Tony McGuinness trophy along with scorer Alan McInally (*left*) and team-mates Pat Bonner and Peter Grant, after the victory against Manchester United

the cameraderie which still exists between these elite players after so many years.'

We had a series of speeches – four of them from that sporting grandfather, Jimmy Johnstone, who joked about the great campaign. Yes, and we had a few tears, too, brushed away as we remembered above all the one man who could not be with us, the architect of the success, the late Celtic manager, Jock Stein.

His two successors Billy McNeill and Davie Hay (who was only a Parkhead cub at the time of Lisbon) were there and Billy paid a graceful tribute to their former boss when he said: 'He was the one who pulled it all together.'

Celtic chairman Jack McGinn and directors Kevin Kelly, James Farrell (the only member of the board who survives from the time of Lisbon), Chris White and Tom Grant were also present to pay their tributes.

From the back-room staff came Bob Rooney, Neil Mochan and Jim Steel – the last two happily still connected with the club.

Record Sports Editor Charles Smith pointed out in his opening speech that Celtic had won the European Cup with eleven

Scottish players, a rare feat for any team to capture the premier club award with native-born players.

There were other occasions, too, when the side were together, notably for an hour-long documentary programme on Scottish television called 'A Pride of Lions'. The black-and-white newsreel pictures showed yet again to a new generation of fans the goals so many of us can instantly recall from memory.

And, of course, there were the personal memories of the players. Defensive anchor-man John Clark, now manager of Clyde, recalled: 'We were walking up the tunnel to the pitch to play Inter Milan, with the Italians beside us.

'They were staring at us for they couldn't believe what was happening. We were cracking jokes and singing the Celtic song. The Italians thought we were demented.'

Right-back Jim Craig, now a dentist, remembered the eve of the Final, when they had gone to spend a few hours at the home of an expatriate Glaswegian businessman at their headquarters in Estoril.

'Someone on the back-room staff said he knew of a short-cut back to the hotel instead of going by the road. We ended up having to scramble down a hill and climb over a fence to get back to the hotel. And this was on the eve of the most important match of our lives.'

Tommy Gemmell remembered the goal he scored – the long-range shot for the equalizer which simply streaked past Milan keeper Sarti. The move was started when right-back Craig darted upfield and put a cross-field pass into the path of the onrushing Gemmell.

Said Tommy: 'Jock Stein had laid down the law that the two full-backs were never to go upfield together. The strict order was if one was up, then one was back.

'When the ball came across it could have rebounded on us if one of their defenders had had enough bottle.

'When he saw me shaping to shoot he came out, but then turned sideways. If he had taken just one more step my shot would have been blocked.

'Then the ball might have ended up at our end of the park and they could have scored a second. With only fifteen minutes to go it would have made it very, very difficult for us. Who would have got the stick then? I would have been the villain and not the hero.'

Gemmell, now part-time manager of Albion Rovers, said: 'I caught the ball beautifully. It just about uprooted the net, and after that there was only going to be one winner.'

Tommy insists a final score of 6–1 in Celtic's favour rather than 2–1 would have been right. 'After they scored with the penalty

Pre-match handshakes from the skippers, Roy Aitken and Bryan Robson of Manchester United, watched by the mascot and referee Alan Ferguson

Pre-match salute, as Roy Aitken acknowledges the cheers of the Celtic
fans

they allowed us to come at them. Sarti put up a show in the Inter
Milan goal I don't think you'll ever see again in a European Cup
Final.

'He was absolutely superb and had saves that came from a
different planet. Ironically, two weeks later he played in an Italian
Cup tie against a Second Division side and he threw two in the
back of the net. He never played for Inter Milan again. That's how
fickle the Italians can be.'

The passage of time meant that many of the eulogy pieces were
penned or spoken by people who were nearer to Largs than Lisbon
on that evening in 1967. It gave rise to some incredible

After match lap of honour, as Roy Aitken shows the fans the trophy

inaccuracies, such as the English newspaper which credited Steve Chalmers' winning goal as a score in extra time instead of near the end of the regulation ninety minutes. Still, mistakes like that cannot alter the real Lisbon story. As John Clark said: 'It's a long time since we all got together. Maybe we should do it more often.'

Let's hope they don't have to wait until 2007 to repeat it!

Just for the record when they met again last May their occupations then were: keeper Ronnie Simpson, publican in Edinburgh, member of the pools panel; Jim Craig, dentist also part-time radio football reporter; Tommy Gemmell, investment consultant and part-time manager, Albion Rovers; Bobby Murdoch, publican in Rutherglen; Billy McNeill, recently left Aston Villa, shortly to become the new Celtic manager; John Clark, manager of Clyde.

Jimmy Johnstone works for a gas installation firm and is part-time youth coach at Celtic. Willie Wallace works for a sports goods manufacturer in Australia; Steve Chalmers is sales manager, Celtic Pools, Bertie Auld, publican in Hamilton, Bobby Lennox, Celtic's reserve team coach.

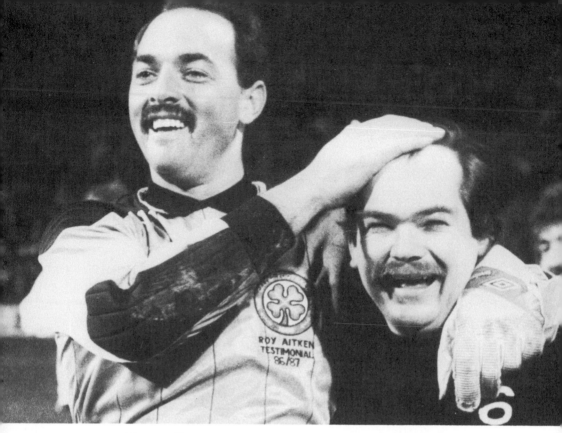

Liverpool keeper Bruce Grobbelaar, after his guest spot at half-time in Roy Aitken's testimonial game, congratulates the winner of the penalty-kick competition

The Lisbon Lions celebrations were essentially private functions, even though the TV cameras were allowed to peek in at one of them. Roy Aitken's celebration was a public event, shared with 36,000 loyal fans who turned up on a mid-week night in March to honour the Celtic captain in his testimonial game. It was the climax to a series of events, including a memorable dinner in the Albany Hotel, Glasgow.

The opponents in the game were Manchester United, whose manager Alex Ferguson paid a massive compliment to Roy when he said: 'He's the biggest single influence on the Celtic side. In fact I can give him no higher accolade than to say he was a bloody nuisance against us at Aberdeen when I was the manager. But I know when I was coach and then manager of Scotland's international side what a great guy he is to have on your side.'

Jokingly he added: 'I expect I'll get my usual welcome from the Jungle. They usually give me pelters. Maybe it's because Aberdeen had a fair record of success against Celtic.'

The tributes to Roy were as sincere as the ones which flowed

The scoring lions of Lisbon on the merry-go-round again . . . as Tommy
Gemmell and Steve Chalmers met former Rangers players Colin Stein
and Davie Provan, with glamour girl Linda McShane keeping order

towards his famous predecessors in the Celtic squad. In a rare honour to one of their on-the-field opponents even title rivals, Rangers, placed an advert in the match magazine.

The teams competed for a trophy, the Tony McGuinness Cup, generously donated by one of the members of the testimonial committee and a well-known Glasgow businessman. And it was Celtic who kept the silverware at Parkhead, with a goal in four minutes appropriately started with a move by Aitken on to Brian McClair, who turned it into the path of Alan McInally to thunder the ball past Manchester United keeper Gary Walsh.

Said Roy at the end of the game: 'It was a tremendous night for me. What a boost it was to see so many fans at the match, and to hear their cheers especially for me. I thoroughly appreciate what has been done for me.'

In his newspaper column Roy had earlier looked back on twelve years at Parkhead and picked the best Celtic team of his time at the club. The line-up is Pat Bonner, Danny McGrain, Pat Stanton, Roy Aitken, Andy Lynch; Paul McStay, Tommy Burns; Davie Provan, Kenny Dalglish, Charlie Nicholas and Bobby Lennox.

Roy admitted: 'The big snag is who to leave out. I'd have Kenny Dalglish and Charlie Nicholas spearheading the attack, and I'd have Davie Provan and Bobby Lennox on the flanks.

'Kenny and Charlie are the two best strikers I've ever seen in a green-and-white jersey, and that's taking nothing away from Brian McClair and Mo Johnston.

'Kenny's class speaks for itself, and Charlie was the sort of striker who created as well as took chances from anywhere in and around the penalty box.'

Expanding further, he said: 'People always have their own ideas but my side would be strong and pacey at the back, inventive and creative in midfield and deadly up front with a winger.

'To fill that bill I would select Pat Bonner, Danny McGrain, Andy Lynch and myself for the defence. And in the middle of the park Paul McStay and Tommy Burns, with wee Lennox making those defence splitting runs from deep positions.'

He also looked back on the game he counts the highlight of his Celtic career – a winning one for the Parkhead team in an Old Firm game.

'We had to beat Rangers in the last match of the 1978–79 season to win the title. We were a goal down and reduced to ten men when Johnny Doyle was ordered off in the second half. But we fought back magnificently to gain a 4–2 victory which clinched the League title for us.'

Some result . . . some night!

THE MAN RANGERS COULDN'T SIGN

Jimmy Steel is unique in Scottish football – he's the man Graeme Souness could not sign for Rangers. If the transfer had gone through it would have been the biggest sensation of them all, an Ibrox snatch from Celtic.

Few of the public may know his name, but such a switch would have created shock waves inside the game for everybody in football knows the man affectionately tagged 'Steely'. Steel is officially the masseur for Celtic, and the Scotland international squad. He has held that post at Parkhead for more than forty years, and a similar role with the SFA for the best part of sixteen years.

It was during the World Cup that Rangers newly appointed manager Graeme Souness and his assistant Walter Smith approached Steel quietly about a possible change from Parkhead to Ibrox. But Jimmy laughed it off by saying: 'I don't want my house burned down.' However he still numbers Souness as a good friend and one of the many amazing facts about this unique man – surely one of football's irreplaceables – is that he has a passport to both Celtic and Rangers dressing-rooms before an Old Firm game. Few can claim such distinction – in fact the only other person I can think of would be the match referee – and certainly no one else is such a welcome guest.

Jimmy Steel, a seventy-three-year-old retired draper from Larkhall, knows more of the secrets of the top players in Scotland than anyone else. He is the person to whom they confide their worries and problems, knowing they are safe with him. Steel is also the jovial joker of the pack, with a set of routines which a top comedian might envy as he soothes away tensions by helping the players relax with laughter.

Jimmy has been associated with the Scotland team since the reign of Tommy Docherty back in the early seventies. 'He has a way with players. He can get them all in the right mood,' said the Doc.

Although he was not part of Willie Ormond's back-room squad he was brought back into the international fold by Ally MacLeod, and stayed on to serve under Jock Stein, then Alex Ferguson and now Andy Roxburgh.

His service with Scotland was marked by a special ceremony at a hotel in Troon after the 1987 Scotland–England match at Hampden. Both Roxburgh and SFA secretary Ernie Walker paid tribute to Jimmy at a private ceremony attended by the international squad when he was presented with a painting as a memento. Jimmy admitted: 'I was overwhelmed. When we got to the hotel they told me I was at the top table because it was my night. I thought they were kidding, and they were winding me up for a "This if Your Life" shot. I was delighted to accept the present. It really is a beautiful picture of a series of footballers, with superb, accurate artwork.'

It was his second presentation in a few weeks. The first came in the form of a present of a pullover accompanied by a card signed by all the Dundee United players, inscribed with the words 'A Million Thanks'. Jimmy, at the request of manager Jim McLean, had helped out the Tannadice squad during their preparations for the UEFA Cup semi-final against Borussia Moechengladbach. He recalls: 'I knew Jim McLean always arrived at the ground early, so I got there at 8.45 sharp to make sure I arrived before him. I had a chat in his office and he told me the players would come in at thirty-minute intervals to have massage and treatment.

'I stayed as a guest in Jim's home, and for two days I worked at Tannadice from 9 in the morning to 4.30 in the afternoon. Jim wanted me to go with them to West Germany, but I turned down the invitation. I was sure they would go on to the final and it would have meant more involvement, and the Scottish Cup Final was coming up as well.

'I'm sure Jim understood. I was grateful for the invitation, but at my age working with Celtic and Scotland is enough.'

Rangers and Dundee United are not the only clubs who have tried to lure Steely away from Parkhead, either on a permanent or part-time basis, but he has stuck through thick and thin with Celtic, the side he was first introduced to during Jimmy McStay's war-time reign as manager. He helped out Tommy Docherty during Manchester United's preparations for their English Cup Final with Southampton, and the Doc wanted to make it a long-term appointment, and Alex Ferguson was anxious to have him at Pittodrie during his time as Aberdeen manager.

Now he must be the longest-serving backroom man with one club in Scottish football, and it's a position he will carry on under Celtic's new boss, Billy McNeill. As old friends they met only days after Billy's appointment and Jimmy joked: 'When I went to see him I asked for a rise of £2, but he told me I could forget about it.'

The joker in the pack – Jimmy Steel (*centre*) with a 1982 line-up at Celtic Park which includes Tommy Burns on the treatment table as his team-mates congratulate him on his return to the Scotland squad. Left to right: Charlie Nicholas, Paul McStay, Steel, Mark Reid, Roy Aitken, Danny Crainie and physio Brian Scott

It was the kind of conversation only two friends of long-standing could have, for each knew the real point of the patter was that Steely has never taken a penny for his services from Celtic. Jimmy recalls happily: 'He said he wanted to see me at the beginning of the season, and that was good enough for me.'

Certainly in a sport which can sometimes spawn hangers-on Jimmy Steel is at the opposite end of the spectrum. He says simply: 'I work hard. I go there to do a job for that's what it's all about.'

He looks back on his international career with Scotland, and picks out the 1982 campaign for the World Cup in Spain as the highlight. It was a team managed by Jock Stein, with Jim McLean as his assistant and Jimmy said: 'It was an honour working with them. They were hard men who knew what they wanted. I really enjoyed it.'

Steely had sat beside Jock Stein on the bench at all the great moments of his managership of Celtic, and he once said: 'You are better to sit quietly. And if you've got something to say make sure it's intelligent or keep your mouth shut.'

He was there, too, on that saddest night for Scottish football, the night Jock Stein collapsed and died at the end of the World Cup match against Wales at Ninian Park, Cardiff.

Jimmy Steel's connection with professional sport began during the Second World War, when he became trainer to boxer Freddie Mills, who became world light heavyweight champion and was one of the most glamorous names in British sport in those far-off post-war years.

Steel used to give the fighter a massage after every training session and Mills would jump down from the table and, jokingly, would throw a right and then a left. Naturally Jimmy always pulled back, but one day he was too slow and he was caught on the nose. 'I woke later that night in agony, and when I looked in the mirror I saw my nose was broken because it wasn't where it was supposed to be. My right eye was shut, and my jaw was swollen black and blue.'

Maybe that's why although he retains a keen interest in boxing it was professional football that took up any of his spare time after that.

He was a personal friend of one of the greatest names in Celtic history, Sir Robert Kelly, of whom he says fondly: 'He was a very fair man. He listened to what you said. He might not agree with it but he never forgot, and maybe a few weeks later he would quietly come back to the suggestion and tell you there was something in it.

'He was a wonderful person, and a great personality. In my opinion he was Mr Celtic. One of the very few people who didn't want any financial gain through his connection with football. And he always wanted quality for Celtic. That meant good types in the club. He had no time for fellows who were going to let the name of the club down.'

These are the common-sense judgements of a man who has known all that is going on in football, yet whose sense of fun is never far below the surface. Like the famous time he even managed to silence the machine-gun delivery of words by Liverpool's legendary boss, Bill Shankly.

It happened when Shanks had visited Celtic's dressing-room before a European Cup Winners Cup game. The famous Bill never one to scorn the chance of a piece of pre-match games-manship, no doubt intended to worry the Parkhead players with

The Celtic Park tribute to Jock Stein, the man Jimmy Steel knew so well.
The battle honours are the pennants from the five rounds of Stein's most
famous campaign, the 1967 European Champions Cup victory

some of his sayings. Instead he was outgunned by the equally
voluble Steely who told him: 'This dressing-room is buzzing, Mr
Shankly. They can't wait to get out there,' and a few other
homilies in similar style. The silenced Shanks for once retreated
back to his own team's dressing-room.

Jimmy Steel's first association with the Scotland team included
the 1972 trip to Brazil for the Copa Independence, the mini World
Cup. I remember from that long, tiring trip how popular he was
with the players, and at the finish of the tour they showed their
appreciation by presenting him with a gold watch.

His room, then as now, was always the meeting place for the
players and Jimmy remembers: 'Some of the boys would be

Manchester United, the team Jimmy Steel could have joined, line up to salute the crowd at the end of the Roy Aitken testimonial match

getting a massage. Billy Bremner would have a card school going. Denis Law would be playing dominoes with some of the others, and phoning room service all the time for those endless cups of tea he drinks!

The only difference now is that a new generation have taken over, but Steel remains, dispensing racing tips from his vast knowledge of his other great love, defending the modern player against accusations of slackness, a real friend to all at either club or country level.

Long may he continue, for he really is a one off. When they made him they broke the mould. He cannot be replaced.